Royal Icing Cookies

45+ Techniques for Stunning & Delicious Edible Art

Morgan Beck

stashBOOKS
an imprint of C&T Publishing

Text copyright © 2023 by Morgan Beck

Photography copyright © 2023 by Morgan Beck

Artwork copyright © 2023 by C&T Publishing, Inc.

PUBLISHER: Amy Barrett-Daffin

CREATIVE DIRECTOR: Gailen Runge

SENIOR EDITOR: Roxane Cerda

EDITOR: Madison Moore

COVER/BOOK DESIGNER: April Mostek

PRODUCTION COORDINATOR: Tim Manibusan

ILLUSTRATOR: Kirstie Pettersen

PHOTOGRAPHY COORDINATOR: Rachel Ackley

FRONT COVER PHOTOGRAPHY by Morgan Beck

PHOTOGRAPHY by Morgan Beck, unless otherwise noted

Published by Stash Books, an imprint of C&T Publishing, Inc., P.O. Box 1456, Lafayette, CA 94549

Attention Teachers: C&T Publishing, Inc., encourages the use of our books as texts for teaching. You can find lesson plans for many of our titles at ctpub.com or contact us at ctinfo@ctpub.com.

We take great care to ensure that the information included in our products is accurate and presented in good faith, but no warranty is provided, nor are results guaranteed. Having no control over the choices of materials or procedures used, neither the author nor C&T Publishing, Inc., shall have any liability to any person or entity with respect to any loss or damage caused directly or indirectly by the information contained in this book. For your convenience, we post an up-to-date listing of corrections on our website (ctpub.com). If a correction is not already noted, please contact our customer service department at ctinfo@ctpub.com or P.O. Box 1456, Lafayette, CA 94549.

Trademark (™) and registered trademark (®) names are used throughout this book. Rather than use the symbols with every occurrence of a trademark or registered trademark name, we are using the names only in the editorial fashion and to the benefit of the owner, with no intention of infringement.

Library of Congress Cataloging-in-Publication Data

Names: Beck, Morgan, 1993- author.

Title: Royal icing cookies : 45+ techniques for stunning and delicious

edible art / Morgan Beck.

Description: Lafayette, CA : Stash Books, an imprint of C&T Publishing,

[2023] | Summary: "Create perfect, stunning cookies that sweeten any

occasion. Included inside are easy-to-follow and tasty recipes for

baking cookies and whipping up a batch of icing. Explore more than 45

techniques and themes to practice before sharing a batch that will

surely be everyone's favorite dessert"-- Provided by publisher.

Identifiers: LCCN 2023004168 | ISBN 9781644033272 (trade paperback) | ISBN

9781644033890 (ebook)

Subjects: LCSH: Cookies. | Cake decorating. | Icings (Confectionery) |

LCGFT: Cookbooks.

Classification: LCC TX772 .B43 2023 | DDC 641.86/54--dc23/eng/
20230207

LC record available at https://lccn.loc.gov/2023004168

Printed in China

10 9 8 7 6 5 4 3 2 1

To those who say, "They're too pretty to eat."

And a little more to those who say "Yum" once they do.

But most of all to NB, GY, EW, MM,
AMS, BRS, and always, Mom and Dad.

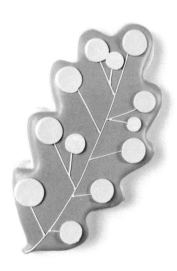

CONTENTS

Introduction
to Cookie Decorating

Cookie decorating is a unique (not to mention yummy!) form of art. Like all forms of art, decorating cookies is a creative outlet and a fulfilling way to express yourself and explore your own artistic style. But unlike many forms of art, it's not meant to last. Because of this, I find that there's an added level of appreciation of the time, detail, and thought put into something that is created to disappear. Why bother putting so much time and effort into something like that?

Well, that's precisely where the difference lies between any old cookie and royal icing art cookies (ahem, notice how many times I've used the word *art* already). The ways in which royal icing can be manipulated, layered, and transformed are endless and exciting; royal icing is truly a delicious clay to be molded.

Baking was an escape for me before it was a regular hobby and eventually a career. It was a way to not be in front of a screen for a few moments. A way to physically make something with my hands. A way to experiment with flavors, with icing techniques, and with colors and textures. And a way to learn from the trial-and-error process (oftentimes heavy on the error). Before long, I was hooked for the long haul.

Beautifully decorated royal icing cookies not only serve as a form of art and expression for the maker but can take any special event to the next level or make a one-of-a-kind gift. A little thoughtful surprise for someone who needs a smile or favors at a wedding reception. No two decorated cookies are ever the same, which makes them so delightfully personal and custom.

Though this book will include step-by-step instructions for many specific cookie designs, it also gives you the tools, techniques, and pointers that will allow you to create your very own one-of-a-kind decorated royal icing cookies. Find inspiration all around you. Notice the textures you see in architecture, the different patterns in fabrics, the shapes of signage when you're walking through town, or the colors in nature. Wonder how they could translate to cookies or be replicated in icing. The ways in which royal icing can be transformed are as endless as the imagination; so start imagining.

In no time, you'll look at the world around you and think, "I could totally cookie that."

Terms and Stuff

Before you bust out those piping bags, there are a few key terms with which to become familiar.

What Exactly Is Royal Icing?

Royal icing is a form of water-based icing made with dried egg whites (meringue powder) and powdered sugar. It's silky smooth in appearance, it's sweet in taste, and it dries hard, which allows for layers upon layers of stable decorative details.

Flooding

To flood a cookie with royal icing means to fill a designated space with a loose-consistency royal icing, which will dry smooth and flat. This is the process used for the base layer of most cookie designs, as it essentially results in an icing canvas.

Outlining

An icing outline is the very thin line of icing piped around the border (or a designated section) of a cookie before it is flooded with icing. The outline forms a barrier that prevents the loose, flood-consistency icing from spilling over the edge of the outlined shape.

Color Bleeding

The color of an icing detail on the cookie seeping into an adjacent area of icing is called color bleeding. This may occur if the first section of icing has not dried fully when the neighboring icing area is applied.

Royal Icing Drying Times

Royal icing is dense with moisture and takes time (and the baker's patience) to dry completely. An average-size cookie (about 3″–4″) with a flood layer of icing will take about 10 to 12 hours to dry completely. Smaller cookie sizes and smaller detailed areas will take less time. When letting cookies dry, a small fan on a low setting may be used to expedite the drying process a bit. Thicker-consistency royal icing will also take less time, as there is less moisture than in a flood-consistency icing. It may sound complicated at first, but you'll get the feel for drying in no time. And until you do, consider the advised drying times that are mentioned in each project throughout this book.

There are a couple stages of drying that are important to consider:

Crusted Over: As quickly as 15–30 minutes after flooding, royal icing may begin to appear hardened on the top. However, the icing underneath will still be quite wet. If you move a crusted-over iced cookie too quickly, the top layer may crack or cave in due to the liquidity of the icing under the surface.

Set: Royal icing takes 3 to 4 hours to set. This means that the icing has hardened enough that the underneath is solid and moving the cookie won't crack or affect the surface. But the icing still retains enough moisture that applying thick layers of detail may cave it in or cause color bleeding. It also may become sticky if packaged in a cellophane bag too soon.

Baking and Decorating Tools

There are several tools that you'll need to decorate almost every cookie you make. There are also some tools used much more sparingly that are unique, if not even odd (looking at you, Bubble Wrap). Be sure you have at least the basic items (and the baking tools) on hand before jumping in!

The Basics

You'll want these at the ready!

- Scribe Scraper tool: This is a plastic tool on which one end comes to a fine point and the other is a flattened scraper. The specific tool I use is called the Thingamagenie and is made by Genie brand. You'll want to keep this handy little tool nearby at all times, as it can be helpful with evenly flooding and scraping away mistakes.

- Disposable piping bags, 10″ size

- Scissors

- Edible ink pens: These pens can write directly onto icing for fine detail. I use Tweets Cookie Connection brand pens.

- Edible ink markers: These markers can color directly onto icing for larger colored sections. I use Chefmaster brand markers.

- Various sizes of paint brushes

- Mixing bowls and spoons

- Gel food color: I prefer using gel colors from the AmeriColor brand.

TYPES OF PIPING BAGS
There are several ways to pipe icing (using metal piping tips, plastic squeeze bottles, reusable silicone bags, etc.), but this book uses disposable piping bags without any piping tips or attachments. Being able to cut the bag tips allows for the hole-size flexibility needed to achieve complex icing designs!

Pretty Common

These tools will come up a few times!

- Silicone Scraper tool: This is a wide, flat silicone tool meant to spread icing smoothly over a large space of cookie. I use the Icing Genie tool from Genie brand.
- Decorative stencils: These are thin, plastic stencils typically between 4″–6″, just big enough to cover a cookie!
- Wax paper
- Parchment paper
- Plastic palette knives, in a variety of shapes and sizes
- Gold and silver metallic luster dust: This is edible metallic color that can be brushed onto icing after being mixed with lemon extract. I use The Sugar Art brand.

The Odd Stuff

You'll need these only once or twice for projects in this book.

- Bubble Wrap
- Clear rock candy
- Metal scribe tool
- Edible glitter spray

Baking Tools

Baking tools are essential for crafting the perfect cookie to decorate!

- Standing mixer with a whisk attachment
- Cookie sheet
- Silicone baking mat: I use a mat from the Chua Cookie brand.
- Measuring cups and spoons
- Wax paper
- Rolling pin
- Cooling racks
- Cookie lifter
- Cookie cutters (the fun part!)

Cookie Cutters 101

There are oodles of cookie cutters out there, and while that's exciting, it can also be intimidating when deciding which to pick. These are some things I like to keep in mind when purchasing cookie cutters:

- Metal cookie cutters often give very sharp, clean edges when cutting dough. However, if they are not cleaned and stored carefully, they may rust or get bent.
- Plastic cookie cutters are becoming more and more accessible as 3D printers are becoming household objects. There are many shops online, specifically through Etsy, that design their own shapes and print their own cutters. These cutters are wonderful because they're very thoughtfully designed and tend to stand out from similar cutters you might find in chain stores. They also hold up very well after many uses—just be careful not to put them in the dishwasher, as the heat may melt and reshape the plastic!
- A standard cookie size is about 4″, but with a caveat. You'll notice when purchasing cutters online that you can often select the size you'd like. The size listed is the longest dimension. If a shape is particularly long and skinny, a 4″ size will appear much smaller than a 4″ square or circle.
- Mini cookies are usually around 2″. If they are much smaller, it becomes difficult to add fine detailing!
- Can't find a cutter you want? Every now and then, you may want to make a cookie shape so specific that it just can't be bought (your friend's dog, your own logo, a unique building in your neighborhood, etc.). While some online shops will work with you to create a custom cutter, you also can use a craft knife, like an X-ACTO, to bring your unique shape to life. Simply print or draw the design on a thick piece of paper, to the size you'd like, and cut the shape out with scissors. Then, on a cutting board, place the cut paper shape onto the rolled-out dough, and carefully cut around it with the craft knife.

Cookie Dough

T his tried-and-true sugar cookie recipe results in a soft, flavorful cookie with minimal spread—perfect for holding cut-out shapes! Make sure to have the baking tools from the previous chapter on hand. This recipe will make about 13 to 15 standard-size cookies.

Vanilla-Almond Sugar Cookie Recipe

Ingredients

- 3 cups all-purpose flour
- ½ tsp salt
- 2 tsp baking powder
- 1 cup unsalted butter, room temperature
- 1 cup granulated sugar
- 1 egg
- 1 tsp vanilla extract
- ½ tsp almond extract

NOTES ON INGREDIENTS
I use Watkins brand extract for both vanilla and almond flavoring.

Instructions

1 Preheat the oven to 350° F. Prepare a cookie sheet with a silicone baking mat.

2 In a medium bowl, combine the flour, salt, and baking powder. Set aside.

3 In the bowl of a stand mixer with a whisk attachment, beat the butter and sugar together until light and creamy, 1–2 minutes. Scrape the sides with a spatula as needed. **A**

4 Add the egg and extracts to the bowl. Mix until fully incorporated.

5 Add the flour mixture to the bowl. Mix until dough forms. **B**

6 Roll the dough out to about ½″ thick between a folded sheet of wax paper. **C**

7 Cut out desired shapes with cookie cutters, and arrange them on the cookie sheet, leaving at least 1″ of space between each cookie. Leave the bottom sheet of wax paper beneath the dough while cutting, then flip the wax paper over to release the dough while keeping it inside the cutter. Then set the cutter with dough inside directly onto the prepared cookie sheet, and lift the cutter up. This transfer method minimizes cookie distortion. **D** **E**

8 Bake for 8–9 minutes or until the center of each cookie has set and no longer looks wet.

9 Remove from the oven, and let the cookies sit on the cookie sheet for 5 minutes before transferring to a cooling rack using a cookie lifter and letting cool completely. **F**

COOKIE BAKE TIMES

Keep in mind that bake times will depend on the size of the dough shapes. Standard-size cookies (3″–4″) will bake for about 8 to 9 minutes, while mini cookies may take only 7 minutes and extra-large cookies may take 12 to 13 minutes. They should just barely start turning a golden brown and no longer look wet in the center when you remove them from the oven. Note that bake times may vary oven to oven, or depending on altitude.

SPREAD

As cookie dough bakes, it tends to expand a little bit, also known as spreading. When baking cookies with intricate shapes, it's important to use a cookie recipe (like the one included in this book!) that results in minimal spreading to ensure the shapes hold. But as a general rule of thumb, it's a good idea to place your shapes of cookie dough an inch apart from each other to allow for any subtle spreading that may occur during the baking process.

Cookie Storage

There are several ways to store cookies, whether they're in the dough stage, they're fully baked cookies, or they're decorated cookies.

Storing Cookie Dough: Prepare the dough as instructed, and roll between sheets of wax paper. Wrap the dough discs fully in plastic wrap, and store in the refrigerator for up to 48 hours. Let the discs sit at room temperature for 15 minutes before cutting shapes.

Storing Baked Cookies: Let baked cookies cool as instructed. After completely cooling and before decorating, you can store baked cookies in an airtight container at room temperature for up to 1 week or in the freezer for up to 3 months.

Storing Decorated Cookies: Fully decorated cookies will stay fresh at room temperature for up to 2 weeks when packaged in individual cellophane bags. They also can be frozen for up to 3 months if you place each individually bagged, decorated cookie in an airtight container. When thawing them out, it's important to keep the lid on the container until it has reached room temperature. This will ensure any condensation takes place outside the container and not on the cellophane bags or the cookies, which may alter the coloring or texture of the icing.

Royal Icing

Royal icing is quick to make, easy to color, simple to store, and yummy to taste: the perfect combination for piping beautiful designs onto your cookies. You'll adjust the icing's consistency based on the cookie design. This recipe will provide enough icing for approximately 2 dozen standard-size, highly detailed cookies.

Royal Icing Recipe

Ingredients

- 6 TBSP meringue powder
- ¾ cups water (plus more for thinning)
- 1 tsp cream of tartar
- 2 tsp clear vanilla
- 8 cups powdered sugar

NOTES ON INGREDIENTS
I use Chefmaster brand meringue powder and Watkins brand vanilla extract. Try Watkins brand clear vanilla extract to keep the icing whiter in color.

Instructions

1 In the mixing bowl of a stand mixer with a whisk attachment, combine the meringue powder and ½ cup of water.

2 Mix on low until combined, scraping the sides with a rubber spatula as needed. Once combined, mix on high until foamy, about the consistency of shaving cream. **A**

3 Add the powdered sugar, cream of tartar, vanilla, and remaining ¼ cup of water. Mix on low until combined, scraping the sides with a rubber spatula as needed.

4 To make the icing thinner, add more water. To make the icing thicker, add more powdered sugar. **B**

Royal Icing Consistency

There are three main icing consistencies: flood, thick, and medium.

Flood-Consistency Icing

Let's start with flood-consistency icing. This is the thinnest or runniest icing consistency, used to fill the top of a cookie with a base layer of icing. I also like to call it "8-second icing." This means that when you lift a spoonful of icing and drizzle it back into the same bowl, it should take about 8 seconds for the drizzled icing to fully smooth back into the icing in the bowl.

Thick-Consistency Icing

Next, let's talk about thick-consistency icing. Don't worry, we'll come back to medium! Thick-consistency icing is used for fine details, like lines, dots, thin lettering, and other delicate decorative elements that need to hold their shape rather than flow or run when piped. When you lift a spoonful of thick-consistency icing from a bowl, it should not be drizzle-able at all!

Medium-Consistency Icing

I like to call medium-consistency icing "miracle icing." Falling somewhere between flood icing and thick icing, medium-consistency icing should be fluid enough that if you work at the icing with a scribe tool, you can make it smooth back into itself, but it can also be used to pipe details with minimal spread. A miracle, I know! By the drizzle test, medium icing may take 12 to 15 seconds to fully smooth back into itself (and may need a little help to get there completely!).

Royal Icing Storage

Royal icing can be stored in an airtight container at room temperature for up to four days. Place a piece of plastic wrap directly onto the surface of the icing before putting the lid on the container. Royal icing can be kept in a piping bag for up to four days as well, though you'll likely notice some natural separation occurring within 24 hours. To resolve, massage the piping bag for about one to two minutes.

It's also simple to freeze royal icing, either in an airtight container or right in the piping bag! Just let it come to room temperature before piping or mixing colors. Royal icing can be frozen for up to two months.

Mixing Colors

To mix colors of icing, you'll need various sizes of mixing bowls, some spoons, and AmeriColor Soft Gel Paste food color. This brand provides quality condensed gels of which a little goes a long way. They are available in dozens of specific colors, which means less color mixing to get the shade you want. Always start by using a small amount of food coloring, and keep in mind that icing will saturate over time. If you're wanting a particularly dark, deep, or rich color, try mixing the color and letting it sit covered overnight. You'll achieve a vibrant color while using less gel color.

2 drops of Deep Pink, 1 Drop of Electric Purple

Color saturation after sitting covered overnight

Filling Piping Bags

To fill a piping bag, hold it in your nondominant hand, and fold the top over your hand an inch or two. Make sure the piping bag does not yet have a hole in the tip. Then use your dominant hand to spoon the icing into the bag. Fill the bag about three-quarters of the way full. Squeeze it down toward the bottom of the bag to bring any air bubbles to the top. Hold the top of the bag, and give it a few good twists to ensure the icing doesn't run out the open end.

How Much Icing Will I Need?

It's important to know how many cookies one piping bag will flood so you can plan ahead, especially if you're mixing specific colors that can be difficult to match perfectly if you need to make more. As a general rule, one 10″ piping bag, filled three-quarters of the way full, will outline and flood about 8 to 9 standard-size cookies.

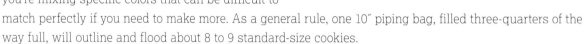

Each project in this book lists just one cookie in each shape as required to make the design. But I'd recommend making a whole batch of cookies and icing to practice with, especially on your first few projects. If you prefer to make smaller batches, you can cut the recipes in half or store the extra dough and icing as noted previously.

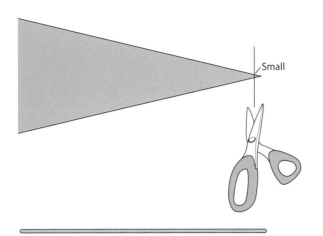

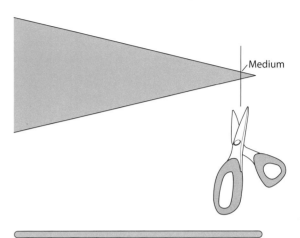

Cutting Piping Bag Tips

Throughout the projects in this book, you'll find instructions about how big or small you'll need to cut the holes in your piping bags. Most commonly, you'll need to cut a small, medium, or large hole, as demonstrated in this graphic. A small cut is used for things like outlining and fine details. A medium cut may be used for larger details or for flooding small shapes. A large cut is most often needed for flooding an entire cookie or large area. As you complete a few projects, you'll start to get the feel for the benefits of different sizes of tip holes!

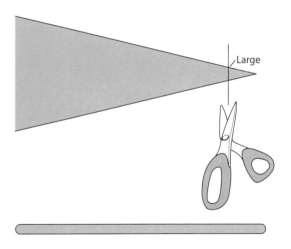

▓ TIP! ▓

Start smaller than you think you need! You can always cut a hole larger. Cut a hole too large? No problem! See page 61 to transfer the icing into a fresh piping bag.

Technique Cookies

In this section, we'll nail down basic piping skills by creating our first cookies! We'll practice outlining and flooding three cookie shapes. Let's start by reviewing the big-picture steps.

Preparing to Pipe

Outlining and flooding a cookie are the groundwork for almost all designs. Both parts are done with flood-consistency icing. Fill a piping bag (see Filling Piping Bags, page 18), and cut a small hole in the piping bag tip for the outline. Then, after piping the outline, cut the tip of the same bag a little bit larger for flooding. I prefer to decorate cookies on a layer of wax paper on the table. This keeps the cookies soft, whereas a surface like paper towels may dry them out sooner.

Outlining Detail Shapes

Once a cookie has been flooded and dried, you may find you'll want to pipe a shape onto the icing. In addition, there may be some cookie designs that don't require a full base flood first but instead require separate sections to be outlined and flooded. This process is similar to outlining and flooding the full cookie. Cut a very small hole in the piping bag tip for the outline. Pipe the outline of the shape you want, then cut the tip of the same bag a little bit larger to flood that specific area.

Holding the Piping Bag

It's important to know how to grip the piping bag so you can achieve the smoothest lines and best designs possible. With your dominant hand, hold the largest part of the piping bag in the ball of your palm. Your thumb will go on top of the twisted area. This is the hand you'll use to apply pressure, move the bag, and keep the top twisted as you work.

With your nondominant hand, place one or two fingers toward the tip of the piping bag. This will steady the bag and help gently direct the icing where you'd like it to go with more control.

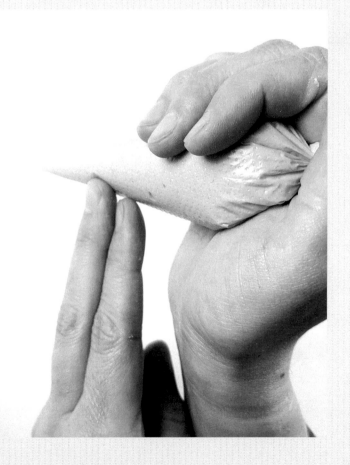

Scribe Scraper Tool

The scribe scraper tool has the potential to be useful in every project. It can help you evenly spread flood icing, and if you make a mistake, you will use it to scrape the icing off the cookie. Keep it on hand at all times!

Square Gift Cookie

When outlining and flooding a shape with straight edges, like a square, treat each straight edge as a separate line. Go from corner to corner, lifting the piping bag up, squeezing with consistent pressure, and letting the icing fall into place along the edge of the cookie. As you bring the piping bag down to the opposite corner, release pressure to complete a straight line. We'll practice outlining and flooding with a simple cookie decorated like a present.

Cookie and Icing List

- 1 baked cookie cut in a square shape
- Flood-consistency icing, green
- Thick-consistency icing, red

Additional Materials

- Scribe Scraper tool
- 2 piping bags
- Scissors

NOTES ON PROJECT

Though these instructions are for one baked cookie, it's a great idea to bake a whole batch and practice over and over, especially if this is your first time working with royal icing. You could even bake a batch made of half square cookies and half circle cookies to use on the next project, Circle Smiley Face Cookie (page 25).

Outline the Square

1 Fill the piping bag with the green flood-consistency icing, and cut a small end of the piping bag tip off. **A**

2 Place the piping bag tip at a corner of the cookie. Squeeze the piping bag with consistent pressure, and lift it up, letting the icing stream fall in a line along one straight edge of the cookie. When you reach the next corner, place the piping bag tip down onto the cookie, and release pressure. **B**

3 Pipe the remaining three edges of the square in the same way, starting and ending at each corner. **C**

4 Let the border dry for 5–10 minutes. This lets the outline get hard enough to hold in the loose icing, preventing the flood from flowing over the edge of the cookie.

A

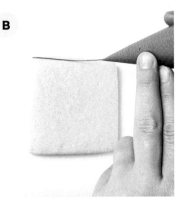

B

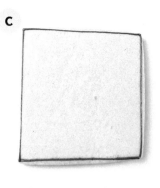

C

■ LET'S TRY THAT AGAIN ■

Piping a line didn't go as planned? Don't sweat it! Use the scraper end of the Scribe Scraper tool to scrape away the unwanted icing. Try again, and remember that practice makes perfect!

Flood the Cookie

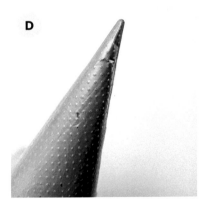

D

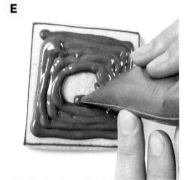

E

1 Cut a slightly larger hole in the tip of the same piping bag. **D**

2 Flood the cookie with icing. Start near the outline, leaving about a ½″ gap around the edge, and use consistent pressure to flood all the way around the cookie, moving inward to the center. **E**

3 Connect the center flood with the outline border by swirling the piping bag in small circular motions, dragging the center out to touch the border. Apply pressure only to add more icing as needed, that is, if the center flood is being stretched too thin to reach the border.

4 Work your way around the cookie in this manner until the center flood has been fully connected to the border. **F**

5 Very carefully, move the cookie side to side, and keeping it flat, tap it up and down in quick short motions. This will incorporate the icing into itself further, giving it a smooth and even flood. This also may bring air bubbles to the surface. Use the Scribe Scraper tool to pop any air bubbles and swirl the icing smoothly back into itself. **G**

F
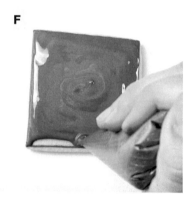

G
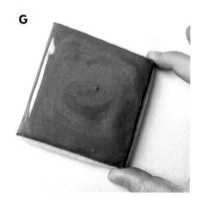

Gift Details

1 Feel free to leave the square as is, or after allowing the cookie to dry completely, fill a bag with the thick-consistency red icing. Cut a small tip off the piping bag.

2 Pipe two or three vertical and a horizontal lines across the center of the cookie. Keep even pressure, and use the same lifted bag technique that you used to pipe the outline. **H**

H

I

3 Pipe a bow in the center of the square where the lines intersect. To create the bow, pipe two ovals above the horizontal line and two wavy lines below the horizontal line, as pictured. Feel free to add multiple lines to make the bow denser. **I**

Circle Smiley Face Cookie

Outlining a circle uses a specific and slightly different technique than outlining straight or decorative shapes. When piping a round shape, let gravity do the work for you. It's not easy to draw a perfect circle, so rather than keeping the piping bag tip close to the cookie, lift the bag up and pipe with consistent pressure, simply guiding the icing as it falls into place around the circle.

Cookie and Icing List

- 1 baked cookie, cut in a circle shape
- Flood-consistency icing, pink
- Medium-consistency icing, black

Additional Materials

- Scribe Scraper tool
- 2 piping bags
- Scissors

NOTES ON PROJECT

Though these instructions are for one baked cookie, it's a great idea to bake a whole batch and practice over and over, especially if this is your first time working with royal icing. You could even bake a batch made of half circle cookies and half square cookies to use on the previous project, Square Gift Cookie (page 22).

Outline the Circle

1 Fill the piping bag with the pink flood-consistency icing, and cut a very small end of the piping bag tip off. **A**

2 Place the piping bag tip at the edge of the cookie. Squeeze with consistent pressure, and lift the piping bag up, letting the icing stream fall into place as you work your way around the edge of the circle. **B**

3 Let the border dry for 5–10 minutes. This will allow the outline to get hard enough to hold in the flooding icing, preventing the flood from flowing over the edge of the cookie.

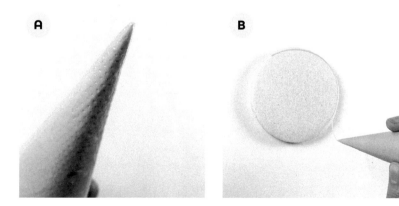

A

B

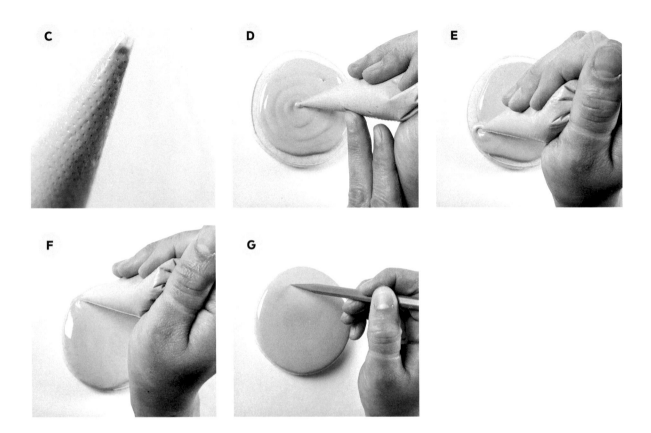

Flood the Cookie

1 Cut a slightly larger hole in the tip of the same piping bag. **C**

2 Flood the cookie with icing. Start near the outline, leaving about a ½″ gap around the edge, and use consistent pressure to flood all the way around the cookie, moving inward to the center. **D**

3 Connect the center flood with the outline by swirling the piping bag in small circular motions, dragging the center out to touch the border. Apply pressure only to add more icing as needed, that is, if the center flood is being stretched too thin to reach the border. **E**

4 Work your way around the cookie in this manner until the center flood has been fully connected to the border. **F**

5 Very carefully, push the cookie side to side, and keeping it flat, tap it up and down in quick short motions. This will incorporate the icing into itself further, giving it a smooth and even flood. This also may bring air bubbles to the surface. Use the Scribe Scraper tool to pop any air bubbles and swirl the icing smoothly back into itself. **G**

Letting the Flood Layer Dry and Packaging

A layer of flooded icing needs sufficient time to dry. Though the top of the icing may appear dry, or crusted over, within 15 to 30 minutes, the icing underneath will remain wet for hours. Allow 10 to 12 hours for a flood layer to dry completely to prevent cracking the icing before it's ready to be decorated further!

If you plan to package a cookie, allow an additional 10 to 12 hours of dry time from your last icing addition before packaging the cookie in a cellophane bag.

Smiley Details

1 Feel free to leave the circle as is, or after allowing the cookie to dry completely, fill a bag with the medium-consistency black icing. Cut a medium sized tip off the piping bag.

2 Pipe two elongated ovals next to each other on the circle to create eyes. Then pipe a thin curved line below to make a smiley face. **H I**

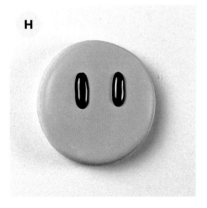

Plaque Wedding Cookie

For cookies that have unique or intricate shapes, pipe closer to the cookie rather than lifting the icing stream and letting it fall into place. As if you were drawing with a pencil on a piece of paper, you'll have more control if you keep the piping bag tip close to the cookie as you outline.

Cookie and Icing List

- 1 baked cookie, cut in an intricate frame or plaque shape
- Flood-consistency icing, blue
- Thick-consistency icing, white

Additional Materials

- Scribe Scraper tool
- 2 piping bags
- Scissors

PLAQUE COOKIE CUTTER
Any frame- or plaque-shaped cutter will work, but the one in this project is from Butter Cutters.

Outline the Plaque

1 Fill the piping bag with the blue flood-consistency icing, and cut a very small end of the piping bag tip off. **A**

2 Place the piping bag tip at one edge of the cookie. Squeeze with consistent pressure, and keep the piping bag tip close to the cookie as you trace around the shape of the cookie. **B**

3 Let the border dry for 5–10 minutes. This will allow the outline to get hard enough to hold in the flooding icing, preventing the flood from flowing over the edge of the cookie.

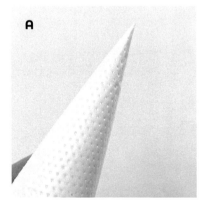

A

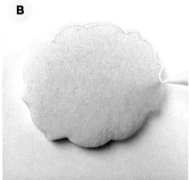

B

Flood the Cookie

1 Cut a slightly larger hole in the tip of the same piping bag.

2 Flood the cookie with icing. Start near the outline, leaving about a ½″ gap around the edge, and use consistent pressure to flood all the way around the cookie, moving inward to the center. **C**

3 Connect the center flood with the outline by swirling the piping bag in small circular motions, dragging the center out to touch the outline. Apply pressure only to add more icing as needed, that is, if the center flood is being stretched too thin to reach the border.

4 Work your way around the cookie in this manner until the center flood has been fully connected to the outline.

5 Very carefully, push the cookie side to side, and keeping it flat, tap it up and down in quick short motions. This will incorporate the icing into itself further, giving it a smooth and even flood. This also may bring air bubbles to the surface. Use the Scribe Scraper tool to pop any air bubbles and swirl the icing smoothly back into itself. **D**

Ring Details

1 Feel free to leave the plaque as is, or after allowing the cookie to dry completely, fill a bag with the thick-consistency white icing. Cut a small tip off the piping bag.

2 Pipe two small, overlapping circles in the center of the cookie. Add a diamond shape to the top of one of the circles to complete a minimalist bridal look. **E**

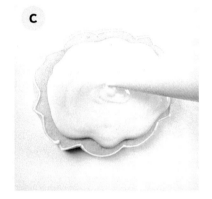

OUTLINING AND FLOODING • PLAQUE WEDDING COOKIE **29**

Wet-on-wet is a flooding technique in which multiple icing colors are added to the flood layer of icing while it's still wet. When the icing dries, this technique results in a smooth, even layer of icing that includes multiple colors. In this chapter, the butterfly, mushroom, and teacup are examples of the wet-on-wet technique.

Similarly, wet-against-wet is the technique of flooding two or more colors *next* to each other in larger sections as opposed to applying multiple wet icing colors on top of one another. The sunset cookie in this chapter is an example of the wet-against-wet technique.

Mushroom Cookie

This cute woodland mushroom design is a great and simple way to introduce the wet-on-wet technique. Try creating a whole forest of different-colored wet-on-wet woodland mushrooms!

Cookie and Icing List

- 1 baked cookie, cut in a mushroom shape
- Flood-consistency icing, red
- Flood-consistency icing, white
- Flood-consistency icing, tan

Additional Materials

- 3 piping bags
- Scissors

MUSHROOM COOKIE CUTTER
Any mushroom-shaped cutter will work, but the one in this project is from Ann Clark Cookie Cutters.

Outline and Flood the Mushroom

1   Fill each piping bag with one of the listed icing colors, and set aside. Using the red icing, outline and flood the mushroom head. For additional guidance, see Outlining and Flooding (page 20). **A**

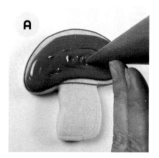

2   Cut a medium-size hole at the end of the white icing piping bag. While the red icing is still wet, add shallow circles of white icing on top of the red. The white circles will sink into the red base flood. Let dry completely, 10–12 hours. **B**

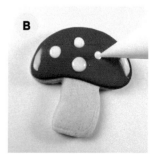

3   Outline and flood the mushroom stem with the tan icing. Let dry completely, 10–12 hours. **C**

Rose Tea Cup Cookie

An endless number of stunning patterns can be made from dragging wet-on-wet flooded icings into intricate shapes with zigzags or swirls. This example will make lovely, dainty, porcelain-style roses!

Cookie and Icing List

- 1 baked cookie, cut in a tea cup shape
- Flood-consistency icing, white
- Medium-consistency icing, pink
- Medium-consistency icing, red
- Medium-consistency icing, green
- Thick-consistency icing, white

Additional Materials

- Scribe Scraper tool
- 5 piping bags
- Small mixing bowl
- Medium paintbrush
- Luster dust, gold
- Lemon extract
- Scissors

TEACUP COOKIE CUTTER
Any teacup-shaped cutter will work, but the one in this project is from Ann Clark Cookie Cutters.

Handle and Base

1   Fill each piping bag with one of the listed icing colors. Cut small holes at the tips of the pink, red, and green icing piping bags, and set aside. When using the wet-on-wet technique, it's a good idea to cut the icing tips ahead of time since you need to work quickly, before the flooded icing starts to harden.

2   Outline the cup, handle, and base of the teacup using the flood-consistency white icing. For additional guidance, see Outlining and Flooding (page 20). **A**

3   Flood the handle and base, leaving the body of the cup blank for now. Let dry for 5–6 hours.

A

B

C

D

E

F

G

4 Mix equal parts gold luster dust and lemon extract in the small mixing bowl using the paintbrush. Brush the gold mixture onto the dried handle and base. **B**

MIXING LUSTER DUST

A little goes a long way with luster dust! You typically only need a dash or two of the dust and a few drops of extract for small surface areas. You can always mix more, and you don't want to waste any of this pricier material.

Flood the Cup

1 Flood the cup section using the flood-consistency white icing.

2 Immediately after flooding, while the icing is still wet, pipe small swirls of pink icing scattered across the cup. Then immediately pipe small swirls of red icing inside the pink swirls. Do not include any swirls in the top quarter-inch of the cup. **C**

3 With the Scribe Scraper tool, swirl the red and pink icings together, dragging some of the white from the flood into each rose. Swirl just 1–2 times to give the rose a natural look and prevent colors from blending too much. **D**

4 While the flood layer and the roses are still wet, pipe small green leaves to the sides of each rose. Put more pressure on the piping bag as you begin piping into the icing, then lighten the pressure as you drag outward. **E**

5 With the Scribe Scraper tool, drag each leaf into a finer point. Let dry until set, about 1–2 hours. **F**

6 Cut a small hole in the tip of the thick consistency white icing, and pipe an elongated oval at the top of the cookie. Let dry completely, about 10–12 hours. **G**

Butterfly Cookie

By swirling multiple icing colors together in this butterfly design, you can create an intricate and beautiful piece of art.

Cookie and Icing List

- 1 baked cookie, cut in a butterfly shape
- Flood-consistency icing, black
- Flood-consistency icing, orange
- Flood-consistency icing, yellow
- Medium-consistency icing, white

Additional Materials

- Scribe Scraper tool
- 4 piping bags
- Scissors

BUTTERFLY COOKIE CUTTER
Any butterfly-shaped cutter will work, but the one in this project is from The Cookiery.

Outline the Sections

1 Fill each piping bag with one of the listed icing colors, and set aside.

2 Cut a small hole at the tip of the black icing piping bag. Outline an elongated oval in the center of the cookie for the butterfly's body.

3 Outline the butterfly's wings in four sections, two on each side. The top sections should be larger than the bottom sections.

4 Pipe two antennas above the body. **A**

Flood the Wings

1 Cut medium-size holes at the tips of the yellow, orange, and black icing piping bags. Pipe a blob of flood-consistency yellow icing in the center of one of the wing sections. **B**

A

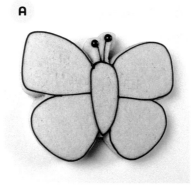

B

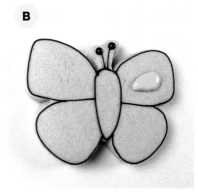

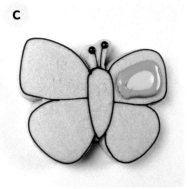

C

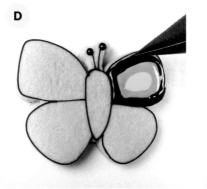

D

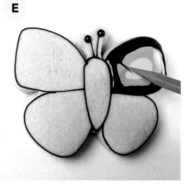

E

F

G

H

2 While the yellow icing is still wet, pipe the flood-consistency orange icing around the yellow icing, leaving a gap of uniced cookie inside the outline. **C**

3 While the orange icing is still wet, pipe the flood-consistency black icing around the orange, connecting the flood to the outline. **D**

4 Drag the Scribe Scraper tool from the black icing inward to the yellow icing, then lift up. **E**

5 Repeat all the way around the wing section. **F**

6 Cut a small hole at the tip of the white icing piping bag. While the icing is still wet, add dots of white icing to the black outer edges. Vary the size of the dots. **G**

7 Repeat Steps 1–6 to decorate the remaining three wing sections. Let dry until crusted over, about 1–2 hours. **H**

Flood the Body

1 Use the black icing to flood the body of the butterfly. **I**

I

Sunset Cookie

This is an example of the wet-against-wet technique, which is created by first outlining the different colored sections and then flooding them one after another so that they will dry smoothly and simultaneously.

Cookie and Icing List

- 1 baked cookie, cut in an arch shape
- Flood-consistency icing, maroon
- Flood-consistency icing, burnt orange
- Flood-consistency icing, peach
- Flood-consistency icing, tan
- Flood-consistency icing, golden yellow

Additional Materials

- 5 piping bags
- Scissors

ARCH COOKIE CUTTER
Any arch-shaped cutter will work, but the one in this project is from KaleidaCuts.

Outline Sunset Sections

1 Fill each piping bag with one of the listed icing colors, and set aside.

2 Cut small holes at the tips of the maroon, burnt orange, peach, and tan icing piping bags. Outline the lowest inch of the cookie, creating a curved line, using the flood-consistency maroon icing. **A**

3 Outline another inch of the cookie with a curved line, above the maroon outline, using the burnt orange icing. You do not need to pipe a line on top of or directly next to the existing maroon line. **B**

A

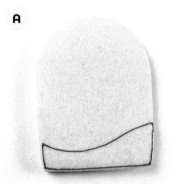

B

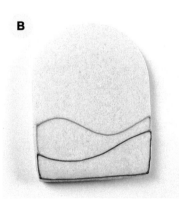

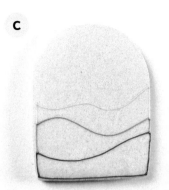

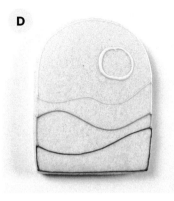

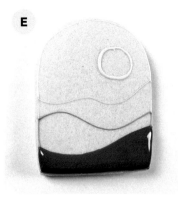

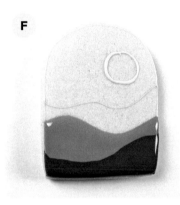

4 Outline another inch of the cookie with a curved line, above the burnt orange icing, using the peach icing. **C**

5 Outline the remainder of the cookie using the tan icing. Outline a circle within the tan section to represent the sun. **D**

Flood the Sunset Sections

1 Cut medium-size holes at the tips of the maroon, burnt orange, peach, tan, and golden yellow icing piping bags. Flood the bottom maroon section using the maroon icing. **E**

2 While the maroon icing is still wet, flood the section above it using the burnt orange icing. Be sure the flooded icings connect completely. **F**

3 While the burnt orange icing is still wet, flood the next highest section with the peach icing. **G**

4 While the peach icing is still wet, flood the remaining section with the tan icing, leaving the circle empty. **H**

5 While the tan icing is still wet, flood the circle with the golden yellow icing. **I**

Piping fine detail lines is a great skill with which to become comfortable. These lines can really give a cookie design that extra *wow* factor! Much like outlining cookies, piping thin lines is done differently depending on the shape and intricacy of the lines.

When piping hard-to-hand-draw lines, such as curves, circles, or straight edges, lift the piping bag tip up, and guide the icing as it falls to produce smoother curves and straighter lines. When piping intricate or detailed lines, keep the piping bag tip closer to the cookie.

Snowflake Cookie

This snowflake design is both simple and elegant. Try making several with different piped line patterns! It'll be great piping practice, and after all, no two snowflakes are the same.

Cookie and Icing List

- 1 baked cookie, cut in a snowflake shape
- Flood-consistency icing, white
- Thick-consistency icing, white

Additional Materials

- 2 piping bags
- Scissors

SNOWFLAKE COOKIE CUTTER
Any snowflake-shaped cutter should work, but the one in this project is from Wilton.

Outline and Flood

1 Fill each piping bag with one of the listed icing colors, and set aside.

2 Outline and flood the cookie using the flood-consistency white icing. Let dry completely, 10–12 hours. **A**

A

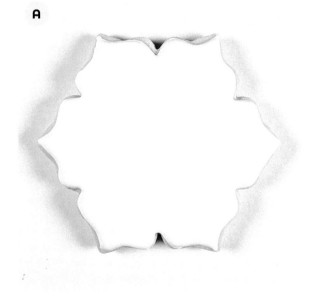

Add the Details

1 Using the thick-consistency white icing, with a small hole at the tip of the piping bag, pipe three straight lines, each going from point to point and intersecting in the middle. **B**

2 Pipe two parallel V shapes, with the wide part of the V closest to the edge of the cookie, at each of the six line tips. **C**

3 Pipe upside-down V shapes in the center of the snowflake, connecting points to form a six-point star. **D**

4 Pipe six dots, one in each section of the snowflake, toward the center of the cookie. **E**

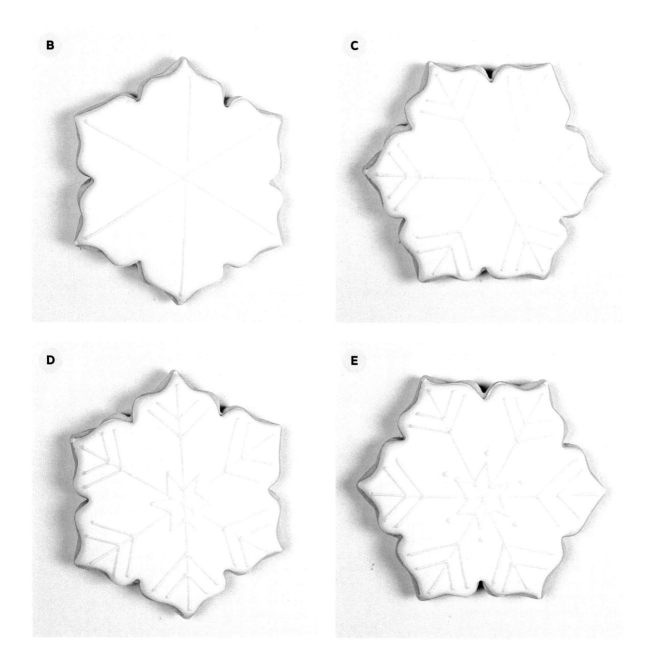

Dog Face Cookie

Get your piping-hand muscles ready—this design includes many layers of fine piped lines to give it a fuller look!

Cookie and Icing List

- 1 baked cookie, cut in a dog face shape
- Flood-consistency icing, white
- Flood-consistency icing, gray
- Thick-consistency icing, white
- Thick-consistency icing, gray
- Thick-consistency icing, black

Additional Materials

- 5 piping bags
- Scissors

DOG FACE COOKIE CUTTER
Any dog face cutter should work, but the one in this project is from Frosted.

Outline and Flood

1 Fill each piping bag with one of the listed icing colors, and set aside.

2 Cut small holes at the tips of the flood white and flood gray icing piping bags. Outline the forehead and mouth region using the flood-consistency white icing. Outline the ears using the flood-consistency gray icing. **A**

3 Cut medium holes at the tips of the flood white and flood gray icing piping bags. Flood the white and gray areas using the wet-against-wet technique (see Sunset Cookie, page 36). Let dry completely, 10–12 hours. **B**

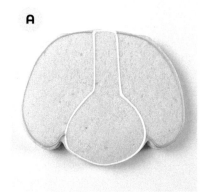

A

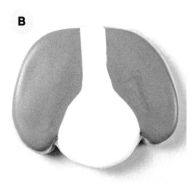

B

Pipe the Dog's White Hair

1 Cut a small hole at the tip of the thick-consistency white icing piping bag. Pipe thin vertical lines from the forehead to the middle of the face using the thick-consistency white icing. Pipe additional lines from the middle of the face down to the chin. **C**

■ **PIPING TIP!** ■

For straight, smooth lines, touch your piping bag tip to the cookie first. Then put pressure on the bag while lifting up. Keeping consistent pressure, carry your icing line to the end point. Touch down, then release pressure.

2 Pipe slightly curved lines from the center of the cookie outward to the right, forming the dog's whiskers. Repeat on the left side. Do not extend the lines over onto the gray ears.

3 Pipe additional lines in the chin area, layering on top of the existing lines to create dimension. Continue layering lines to the whiskers and chin for an extra shaggy look! **D**

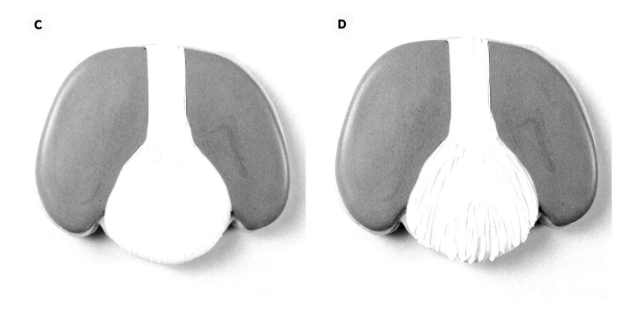

C

D

Pipe the Dog's Gray Hair

1 Cut a small hole at the tip of the thick-consistency gray icing piping bag. Pipe curved lines around the shape of one ear using the thick-consistency gray icing. Start and finish each line near the top of the head. Layer gray lines until you're happy with how full the ear appears. **E**

2 Repeat Step 1 on the other ear. **F**

Add the Dog's Face

1 Cut a small hole at the tip of the thick-consistency black icing piping bag. Pipe a nose using the thick-consistency black icing. The nose should be a small, rounded T shape on top of the white fur, near the center of the cookie.

2 Pipe a black dot where the white and gray fur meet on each side of the face for the eyes. While the icing is still wet, add a small dot of thick-consistency white icing to the top right corner of each eye. **G**

3. Still using the black icing, pipe a small vertical line directly underneath the nose. Add a small curve on either side of the line to form the smile.

4 Using the thick-consistency gray icing, pipe a shaggy line above each eye to form the eyebrows. **H**

Mitten Cookie

This piped woven pattern, made up of straight, curved, and zigzag lines, can be applied to other cookie shapes as well. Try it on a sweater, hat, or plaque shape!

Cookie and Icing List

- 1 baked cookie, cut in a mitten shape
- Flood-consistency icing, maroon
- Thick-consistency icing, maroon
- Flood-consistency icing, light gray

Additional Materials

- 3 piping bags
- Scissors

MITTEN COOKIE CUTTER
Any mitten-shaped cutter will work, but the one in this project is from Ann Clark Cookie Cutters.

Outline and Flood the Hand Section

1   Fill each piping bag with one of the listed icing colors, and set aside.

2   Outline and flood the mitten with the flood-consistency maroon icing, leaving the cuff area blank. Let dry completely, 12–14 hours. **A**

Pipe the Mitten Details

1   Cut a small hole at the tip of the thick-consistency maroon icing piping bag. Pipe four thin, evenly spaced vertical lines down the center of the cookie using the thick-consistency maroon icing. **B**

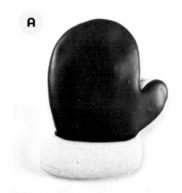

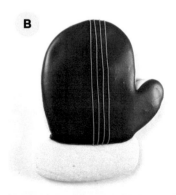

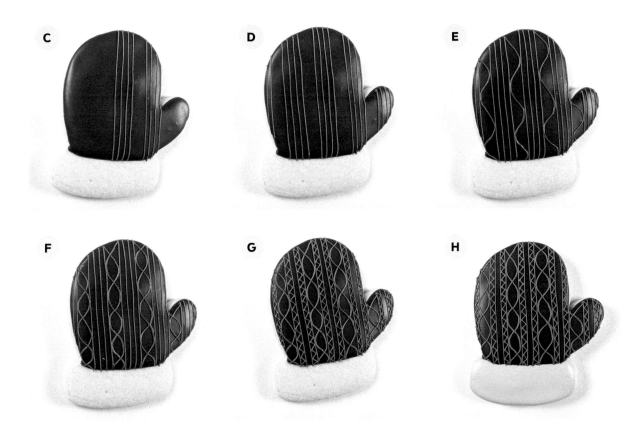

2 Leave a wider gap, then pipe another four thin, evenly spaced vertical lines. **C**

3 Repeat Steps 1–2 across the flooded area, piping lines all the way to the left and right edges of the mitten. **D**

4 In each wide column, pipe a line that curves back and forth like an S from the top to the bottom. Pipe a second curving line in each wide column, curving in the opposite direction so the curves cross over each other. **E F**

5 Pipe zigzags in each skinny column on either side of the wide columns. Leave the remaining skinny columns between the zigzag columns empty. Let the details dry for about 1 hour. **G**

Outline and Flood the Cuff

1 Outline and flood the cuff using the flood-consistency light gray icing. **H**

Funky Rainbow Cookie

This example will involve thin, rounded lines and polka dots. Some will be left as thin strokes, and some will be flooded with icing!

Cookie and Icing List

- 1 baked cookie, cut in a rainbow shape
- Flood-consistency icing, white
- Medium-consistency icing, maroon
- Medium-consistency icing, burnt orange
- Medium-consistency icing, gold
- Medium-consistency icing, peach

Additional Materials

- Edible ink pen, black (optional)
- 5 piping bags
- Scissors

RAINBOW COOKIE CUTTER
Any arch-shaped cutter will work, even a solid arch without a gap in the middle, but the one in this project is from Frosted.

Outline and Flood

1   Fill each piping bag with one of the listed icing colors, and set aside.

2   Outline and flood the cookie with the white icing. Let dry completely, 12–14 hours. **A**

Add the Details

1   Outline and flood an arch shape, about ¼″ thick, near the outer edge of the cookie using the medium-consistency maroon icing. Remember to lift the bag and guide the icing as it falls while piping the curved lines. **B**

TIP!

When flooding thin or skinny areas, try piping a squiggle of icing first, then flooding - this extra icing below the flood will help prevent the icing from denting or caving in as it dries.

2 Use the medium-consistency burnt orange icing, with a small hole at the tip of the piping bag, to pipe an arched line underneath, but not touching, the maroon arch. **C**

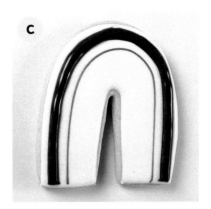

3 Below the burnt orange arch, outline and flood a ¼″-thick arch using the medium-consistency gold icing. **D**

4 Use the medium-consistency peach icing, with a small hole at the tip of the piping bag, to pipe a dotted arch below the gold arch. **E**

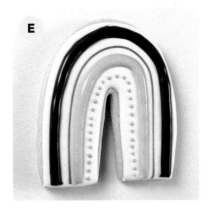

5 After the maroon arch has dried for at least 1 hour, use the medium-consistency peach icing, with a small hole at the tip of the piping bag, to pipe an arched line on top of the maroon arch.

6 OPTIONAL: Add dots in some of the white space with the edible ink pen for a funky touch! **F**

Parchment paper + royal icing = a match made in heaven. Parchment paper has a thin silicone coating, which makes it a nonstick material that can be applied to royal icing after it's been flooded. When the icing dries, the parchment paper comes right off, easy peasy! So many effects can be achieved with a little bit of parchment paper creativity.

Moon and Stars Cookie

By crinkling a sheet of parchment paper, you can achieve a bumpy and textured surface—just like the moon! It's a simple way to add some visual interest to a cookie.

Cookie and Icing List

- 1 baked cookie, cut in a moon shape
- Flood-consistency icing, gray
- Medium-consistency icing, yellow

Additional Materials

- Fine-detail paintbrush
- Piece of parchment paper, 6″ × 6″
- 2 piping bags
- Luster dust, gold
- Lemon extract
- Small mixing bowl

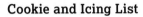

BEFORE YOU BAKE
Don't have a moon-shaped cutter? Try using two sizes of circle cutters!

Prepare the Parchment Paper

1 Crumple the piece of parchment paper into a tight ball. **A**

2 Carefully undo the ball; the result is a crinkly piece of parchment paper. **B**

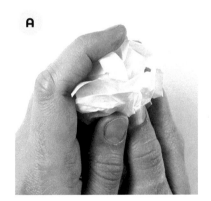

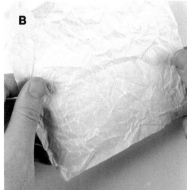

C

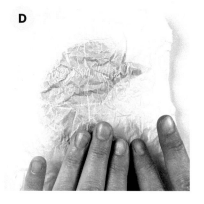

D

E

Outline and Flood

1   Fill each piping bag with one of the listed icing colors, and set aside.

2   Outline and flood the moon using the flood-consistency gray icing. **C**

F

3   While the icing is still wet, place the crinkled piece of parchment paper over the whole cookie. Gently press down on the parchment paper to make sure it's fully adhered to all areas of the flooded cookie. Be careful not to push too hard. Let dry for 10–12 hours. **D**

4   Once the icing is dry, gently peel the parchment paper off of the cookie. **E**

Add the Details

1   Outline three small stars using the medium-consistency yellow icing with a small hole in the tip of the piping bag. Draw them just as you would on a piece of paper. Then cut the piping bag tip a little bit larger, and fill in the stars. Let dry for 1 hour.

2   Mix equal parts gold luster dust with lemon extract in the small mixing bowl using the fine-detail paintbrush.

3   Paint gold onto each star. **F**

Mountain Range Cookie

This technique involves folding the parchment paper like a fan. What other ways can you think of to fold parchment paper for a fun and unique effect?

Cookie and Icing List

- 1 baked cookie, cut in an arch shape
- Flood-consistency icing, dark blue
- Flood-consistency icing, light gray
- Thick-consistency icing, white

Additional Materials

- Medium-size paintbrush
- Luster dust, silver
- Small mixing bowl
- Lemon extract
- Piece of parchment paper, 6″ × 6″
- 3 piping bags
- Tape

ARCH COOKIE CUTTER
Any arch-shaped cutter will work, but the one in this project is from KaleidaCuts.

Outline, Flood, and Sprinkle with Silver

1 Fill each piping bag with one of the listed icing colors, and set aside.

2 Outline and flood the cookie using the flood-consistency dark blue icing. Let dry for 10–12 hours.

3 Mix equal parts silver luster dust and lemon extract in a small mixing bowl using the paintbrush. **A**

4 Hold the paintbrush about 6″to 8″ above the flooded cookie, and tap the brush with your finger, splattering the luster dust mixture onto the icing to achieve the look of a starry night sky. **B**

■ PRACTICE SPLATTER SHEET ■
Before you splatter the food color mix onto your cookie, consider practicing on a paper towel to get the feel for the technique!

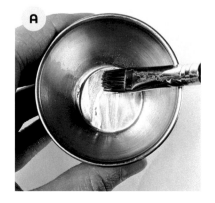

51

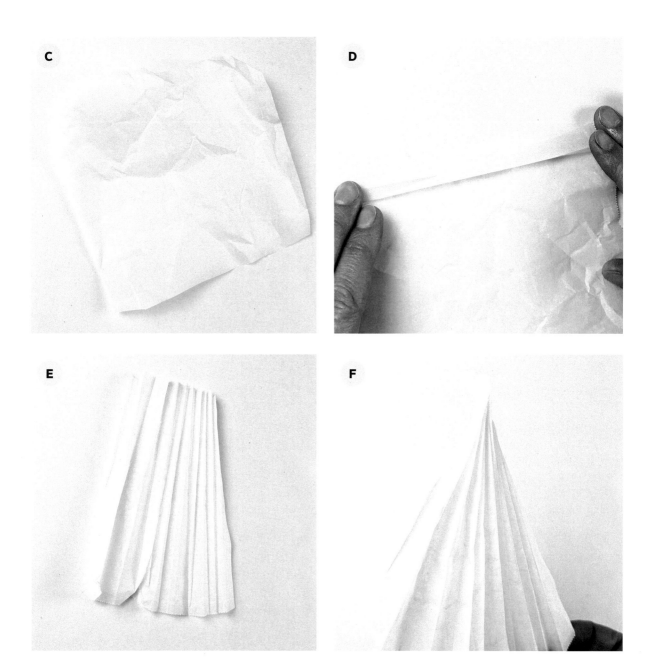

Prepare the Parchment Paper

1   Crumple the piece of parchment paper just slightly to add some creases and texture to it. **C**

2   Starting at one edge, fold the parchment paper over, then back under, in small sections, creating a fan effect. **D E**

3   Tape one end of the parchment paper to form an angled shape. **F**

Outline and Flood the Mountains

1 Outline and flood the mountains. First, using the flood-consistency light gray icing with a small hole at the tip of the piping bag, pipe along the bottom edge of the cookie, then pipe jagged lines for the mountain tops. Cut a slightly larger hole in the same piping bag, and flood the mountain shape. **G**

2 While the icing is still wet, place the piece of parchment paper over the whole cookie.

3 Gently press down on the parchment paper to make sure it's fully adhered to all areas of the flooded cookie. Let dry for 10–12 hours. **H**

4 When the icing is dry, gently peel the parchment paper off of the cookie.

Add Snowy Peaks

1 Use the thick-consistency white icing with a medium-size hole at the tip of the piping bag to drizzle small amounts of white icing on the tips of the mountains.

2 Dab the white icing with the paintbrush to create a soft, snowy look. **I J**

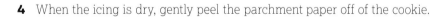

Boho Branch Cookie

Parchment paper doesn't always need to be crumpled or folded first to get a beautiful texture. This example involves a flat sheet of parchment paper and results in a boho, trendy feel. Try this same flat-sheet technique on a full flood layer of icing!

Cookie and Icing List

- 1 baked cookie, cut in a leafy branch shape
- Flood-consistency icing, dusty rose
- Medium-consistency icing, tan

Additional Materials

- Piece of parchment paper
- 2 piping bags

BRANCH COOKIE CUTTER
Any leafy- or branch-shaped cutter will work, but the one in this project is from Ann Clark Cookie Cutters.

Outline and Flood

1 Fill each piping bag with one of the listed icing colors, and set aside.

2 Outline and flood the cookie using the flood-consistency dusty rose icing. Let dry completely, 10–12 hours. **A**

B

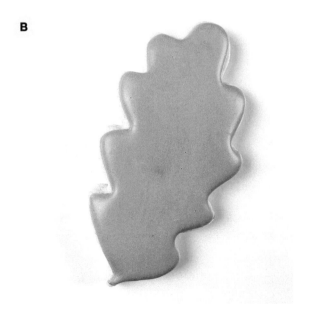

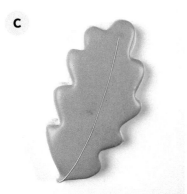

C

D

E

Add the Stem and Leaves

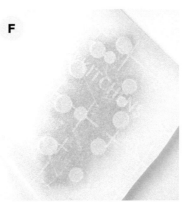

F

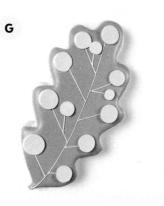

G

1   Cut a small hole at the tip of the medium-consistency tan icing piping bag. Pipe a long stem through the center of the leaf shape. See Fine-Line Piping (page 38) for practice piping. **C**

2   Pipe smaller stems branching out from the main stem, letting the shape of the cookie dictate where the leaves will be. **D**

3   Cut the piping bag tip hole a little larger. Pipe circles at the ends of the short stems. **E**

4   While the circles of icing are still wet, place the sheet of parchment paper over the cookie. Gently press down on the parchment paper to make sure it's fully adhered to the circle areas. Let dry for 10–12 hours. **F**

5   When the icing is dry, gently peel the parchment paper off of the cookie. **G**

◼ VARIETY! ◼

If you're making a batch of these boho branch cookies, add some variety by leaving some of the cookies without parchment paper texture. The mix of flat and round circles will make for a visually interesting set.

Sometimes you just want a cookie to do the talking. There are several styles of lettering that can be achieved with royal icing. Something for every occasion: subtle and dainty or loud and proud.

Lettering might seem daunting at first. Before you take to your perfectly flooded cookie, try doing some practice alphabets first by tracing printouts on parchment paper! Scan this QR code or visit tinyurl.com/11552-patterns-download to access a downloadable practice PDF that includes sheets of letters in various fonts to practice with. Tape a sheet of wax paper over the printed letters, then pipe until you feel confident!

Repeating lettering styles and techniques will give you a better feel for the amount of pressure you need to apply, the size of the hole at the tip of the piping bag, and how you move your hand to achieve lettering you can confidently pipe onto a cookie.

Thin-Script Cookie

A thin script is a nice addition to a cookie design that includes other imagery. It's small but powerful, and the cursive gives it an elegant feel.

Cookie and Icing List

- 1 baked cookie, cut in a rectangular plaque shape
- Flood-consistency icing, dark blue
- Medium-consistency icing, red
- Medium-consistency icing, yellow
- Medium-consistency icing, green
- Medium-consistency icing, light blue
- Thick-consistency icing, white

Additional Materials

- 6 piping bags

RECTANGLE COOKIE CUTTER
Any rectangular-shaped cutter will work, but the scalloped one in this project is from LILIAO.

Outline and Flood

1 Fill each piping bag with one of the listed icing colors, and set aside.

2 Outline and flood the cookie using the flood-consistency dark blue icing. Let dry completely, 12–14 hours.

A

A

Add the Details

1   Cut small holes in the tips of the red, yellow, green, and light blue icing piping bags. Pipe a tall, thin rectangle from the bottom of the cookie up to about the middle of the cookie, starting on the far left edge and using the medium-consistency red icing. Repeat across the bottom of the cookie with the yellow, green, and light blue icings. Alternate colors to create a colorful row of birthday candles. Let them crust over, about 30 minutes. **B**

2   Use the thick-consistency white icing with a small hole at the tip of the piping bag to pipe a short wick at the top of each candle. **C**

3   Pipe a small flame at the top of each wick using the medium-consistency yellow icing. Apply more pressure to the piping bag closer to the wick, letting up on pressure as you drag away from the wick, forming a flame shape. **D**

D

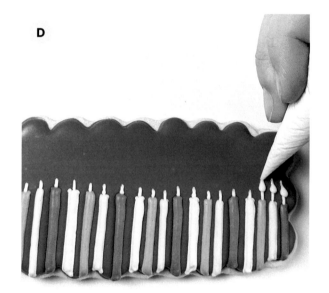

E

F

G

H

Add the Text

1   With a small hole at the tip of the thick-consistency white icing piping bag, start on the left, and pipe the first letter of the text. In this example, we'll write the text *happy birthday to you*, so start with a cursive letter *h*. **E**

2   Lift up and assess spacing after each letter. The beauty of script text is that the connectors between letters can be shortened or elongated based on the amount of space you have and still look natural.

3   Work your way across the cookie letter by letter, saving dots and crosses until the words are finished. **F G**

4   Add any necessary dots and crosses. **H**

Bold-Script Cookie

Bold-script text uses a technique known as "pressure piping." This means that within a single piping motion, you adjust the pressure on the piping bag to produce gradually thicker and thinner strokes.

Cookie and Icing List

- 1 baked cookie, cut in a rectangular plaque shape
- Flood-consistency icing, red
- Medium-consistency icing, yellow

Additional Materials

- 2 piping bags

RECTANGLE COOKIE CUTTER
Any rectangular-shaped cutter will work, but the one in this project is from KaleidaCuts.

Outline and Flood

1 Fill each piping bag with one of the listed icing colors, and set aside.

2 Outline and flood the cookie using the flood-consistency red icing. Let dry completely, 12–14 hours. **A**

Add the Text

1 Cut a medium-size hole in the tip of the medium-consistency yellow icing piping bag, and pipe a lowercase cursive letter c on the left side of the cookie. When piping thick-script text, apply more pressure to the piping bag as you downstroke, creating a thicker bottom portion of each letter. Soften pressure as you upstroke, resulting in thinner top portions. Lift the piping bag up completely after finishing each letter. **B**

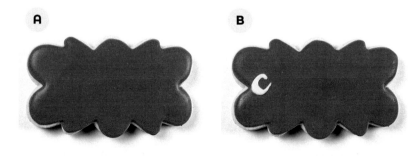

C

D

E

2 Pipe a lowercase cursive letter *o*, attaching it to the tail made from the *c*. Remember to apply more pressure as you downstroke so the bottom of the letter is thicker. **C**

3 Continue, spelling the word *congrats*. **D E F**

F

G

Add the Details

1 Pipe small stars in the space around the text using the medium-consistency yellow icing. **G**

GRAB A NEW PIPING BAG
You might find that the piping bag tip hole size you found comfortable for piping the text is too large for piping finer details like stars in this example. To transfer the icing to a new piping bag, cut a larger hole in the tip of the old bag and squeeze the icing into a new bag. Now you can cut a smaller hole at the new piping bag's tip!

Words or Images First?

How do you know when to start with the text and when to start with the imagery? This will depend on your desired design. Sometimes you'll want the text to be the focal point or most important aspect of a cookie design. In those cases, pipe the text first, and add any supporting details around it afterward. At other times, you'll want imagery to be the spotlight and the text to be secondary. In those cases, create the image you'd like first, with a space for the text in mind.

Thin Sans Serif Cookie

Thin sans serif lettering is a staple. It can be applied to very detailed cookie designs or can make a minimalist statement on its own.

Cookie and Icing List

- 1 baked cookie, cut in a decorative plaque shape
- Flood-consistency icing color, royal blue
- Thick-consistency icing, white
- Thick-consistency icing, yellow

Additional Materials

- 3 piping bags
- Scissors

PLAQUE COOKIE CUTTER
Any frame- or plaque-shaped cutter will work, but the one in this project is from The Bakery Studio.

Outline and Flood

1 Fill each piping bag with one of the listed icing colors, and set aside.

2 Outline and flood the cookie using the flood-consistency royal blue icing. Let dry completely, 12–14 hours. **A**

Add the Text

1 Before you start piping, determine where you want the text to go. Maybe it will be centered, or maybe aligned right or left. In this example, we'll align the text *HAPPY HANUKKAH* at the bottom right of the cookie.

2 With a small hole at the tip of the piping bag, pipe the last letter of the phrase (*H*) at the right bottom corner of the cookie. **B**

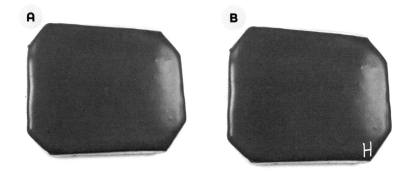

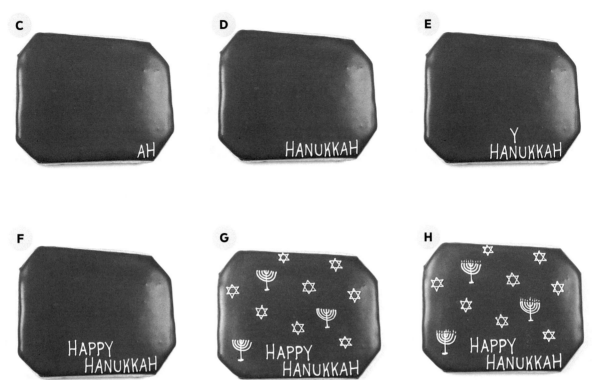

3 Pipe the second-to-last letter (*A*) to the left of the existing letter. Continue working backward until you've completed the word (*HANUKKAH*). **C** **D**

> ■ WRITE IT OUT ■
> When piping a word backward, it's a good idea to write the word out on a piece of paper and keep it near you as you pipe to make sure you're spelling it correctly backward!

4 Determine where you want the first word (*HAPPY*) to sit. In this example, we'll place it a line above *HANUKKAH* and staggered forward a bit. Pipe the last letter (*Y*) where you want the word to end. **E**

5 Pipe the remaining letters from right to left, spelling the word backward. **F**

Add the Details

1 Using the same thick-consistency white icing and piping bag, pipe a pattern of the Star of David and menorahs around the cookie. **G**

2 Pipe small flames at the top of each menorah using the thick-consistency yellow icing. **H**

Bold Sans Serif Cookie

Bold lettering is a fun way to fill the cookie's space and make a statement. These letters are even thick and big enough to have decorations added on top! Try a wet-on-wet pattern, a pen pattern, or fine-line icing stripes on top of the letters.

Cookie and Icing List

- 1 baked cookie, cut in a rectangle shape
- Flood-consistency icing, purple
- Medium-consistency icing, coral
- Medium-consistency icing, lime-green
- Medium-consistency icing, dark pink
- Medium-consistency icing, green
- Medium-consistency icing, tan

Additional Materials

- 6 piping bags
- Scissors

RECTANGLE COOKIE CUTTER
Any rectangular-shaped cutter will work, but the one in this project is from KaleidaCuts.

Outline and Flood

1 Fill each piping bag with one of the listed icing colors, and set aside.

2 Outline and flood the whole cookie using the flood-consistency purple icing. Let dry for 10–12 hours. **A**

START IN THE MIDDLE
When piping a word in the center of a cookie, start with the middle letter in the center of the cookie and work outward to get the spacing right!

A

B

C

D

Outline the Letters

1 Cut small holes at the tips of the dark pink, lime-green, green, coral, and tan icing piping bags.

2 Outline a capital letter *R* using the medium-consistency dark pink icing. Keep in mind that this letter will dictate the height of the rest. **B**

3 Outline a capital letter *A* to the left of the *R* using the medium-consistency lime-green icing, making sure it is the same height.

4 Outline a capital *T* to the right of the *R* using the medium-consistency green icing. **C**

5 Outline a capital *P* to the left of the *A* using the medium-consistency coral icing.

6 Outline a capital *Y* to the right of the *T* using the medium-consistency tan icing. **D**

E

Flood the Letters

1 Cut medium-size holes at the tips of the dark pink, lime-green, green, coral, and tan icing piping bags.

2 Flood each letter using the icing color that matches each outline. **E**

Negative Space Cookie

For a fun twist on lettering with unique dimensionality, form bold letters by flooding around negative space.

Cookie and Icing List

- 1 baked cookie, cut in a circle shape
- Flood-consistency icing, red
- Flood-consistency icing, pink
- Medium-consistency icing, red
- Medium-consistency icing, white

Additional Materials

- 4 piping bags
- Scissors

Outline and Flood

1 Fill each piping bag with one of the listed icing colors, and set aside.

2 Outline and flood the whole cookie using the flood-consistency red icing. Let dry completely, 10–12 hours. **A**

A

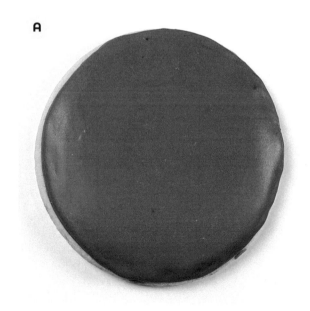

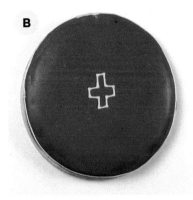

Outline the Letters and Flood

1 Use the flood-consistency pink icing with a small hole cut at the tip of the piping bag to outline around the whole cookie.

2 Outline a plus sign in the center of the cookie. **B**

3 Outline a capital letter to the left and right of the plus sign. This example uses an *E* and a *K*. **C**

4 Cut a slightly larger hole in the same piping bag. Flood the area outside of the letters, connecting to the outer circle outline. Let dry for 10–12 hours. **D E**

Add the Details

1 Using the medium-consistency red and white icings with medium holes at the tips of the piping bags, pipe hearts on top of the pink icing. Apply pressure to the piping bag as you drag down, and release pressure to form half a heart. Repeat on the facing side to complete a heart. **F**

𝒜dding texture to a cookie design can take it to the next level. There are tons of fun ways to achieve textures; see Parchment Paper Texture (page 48) for even more ideas.

Friendly Monster Cookie

This "fuzzy" texture, achieved with a paintbrush, can be applied to all sorts of cookie designs: a teddy bear, a pair of cozy slippers, even the textured ground beneath a dirt bike.

Cookie and Icing List

- 1 baked cookie, cut in a round scalloped shape
- Flood-consistency icing, teal
- Medium-consistency icing, white
- Medium-consistency icing, black
- Medium-consistency icing, teal
- Medium-consistency icing, lime-green

Additional Materials

- Medium-size paintbrush
- Edible ink markers (optional)
- 5 piping bags
- Scissors

Outline and Flood

1 Fill each piping bag with one of the listed icing colors, and set aside.

2 Outline and flood the cookie using the flood-consistency teal icing. Let dry completely, 10–12 hours. **A**

A

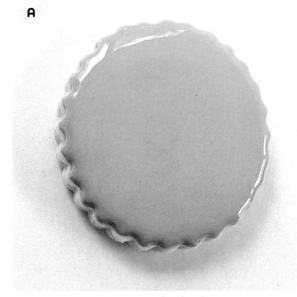

Icing still wet after flooding

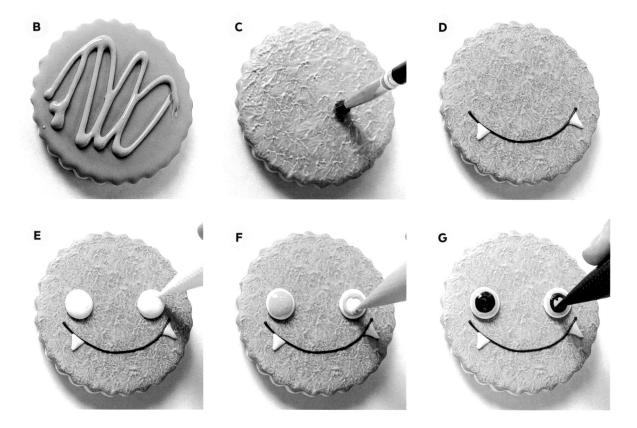

Add the Fuzz

1   From a piping bag with a medium-size hole at the tip, drizzle medium-consistency teal icing on top of the flooded and dried cookie. **B**

2   Dab the icing evenly across the entire cookie with the paintbrush, using quick up-and-down motions. Continue until the icing is evenly distributed and the monster is as fuzzy as you'd like! Let the fuzzy layer dry for 15 minutes. **C**

Add the Mouth

1   Use the medium-consistency black icing with a small hole at the tip of the piping bag to pipe a curved smile on the monster.

2   Use the medium-consistency white icing with a small hole at the tip of the piping bag to pipe a small triangle tooth on either end of the smile. **D**

Add the Eyes

1   Cut a slightly larger hole at the tip of the medium-consistency white icing piping bag. Pipe two round mounds of icing above the mouth for eyes, each about the size of a dime. **E**

2   Cut a medium-size hole at the tip of the medium-consistency lime-green icing piping bag. While the white circles are still wet, add a smaller circle of lime-green icing on top of each eye. **F**

3   Cut a small hole at the tip of the medium-consistency black icing piping bag. While the lime-green circles are still wet, add a smaller circle of black icing on top of each eye. **G**

4 Cut a small hole at the tip of the medium-consistency white icing piping bag. Finish the eyes by adding a small dot of white on the line between the lime-green and black areas. **H**

5 Add an eyebrow above each eye with the black icing. **I**

Add the Bowtie and Antennas

1 Create two thin antennas hanging down from the top of the monster's face with the black icing. Add a circle of lime-green icing to the end of each antenna. **J**

2 Outline and fill two triangles connected at one point at the bottom of the cookie with lime-green to create the monster's bowtie. Let dry for 10 minutes. **K**

3 Add a circle of icing on top of the two triangles, in the middle, to create the center of the bowtie. **L**

4 Once the icing is completely dry, add some marker details to the bowtie, like polka dots or stripes!

Baby Onesie Cookie

This frill technique, created with a paintbrush, adds a lovely lacey look to a cookie design. Try it around the border of a heart for a sweet Valentine's Day cookie!

Cookie and Icing List

- 1 baked cookie, cut in a onesie-with-sleeves shape
- Flood-consistency icing, pink
- Medium-consistency icing, white
- Thick-consistency icing, pink
- Medium-consistency icing, green

Additional Materials

- Round medium paintbrush
- 4 piping bags
- Scissors

ONESIE COOKIE CUTTER
Any cutter shaped like a onesie with short sleeves will work, but the one in this project is from Lolano Cookie Cutters.

Create the Frills

1 Fill each piping bag with one of the listed icing colors, and set aside.

2 Use the medium-consistency white icing with a medium-size hole at the tip of the piping bag to pipe three large dots of icing on the outermost part of one of the sleeves. **A**

3 Push the paintbrush tip down into the center of one icing dot and drag toward the center of the cookie. Repeat for the remaining two icing dots. **B**

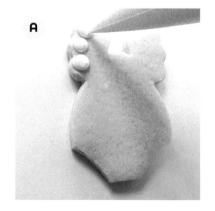

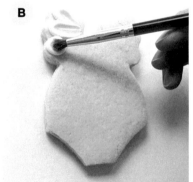

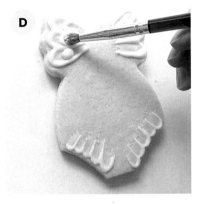

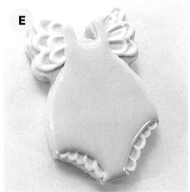

4 Repeat Steps 2–3 on the other sleeve. Let the frills dry for 15 minutes.

5 While you're waiting, add five smaller dots around each leg curve and brush inward to create smaller frills. **C**

6 When the sleeve frills have hardened, give them a little more dimension by repeating this technique (Steps 2–3) on top of the existing frills. Place the dots a little more inward on the cookie. Allow this second layer of frills to dry for 15 minutes. **D**

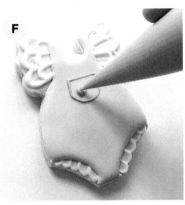

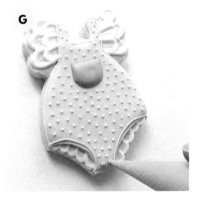

Outline and Flood

1 Outline and flood the remaining uniced area of the cookie with flood-consistency pink icing, making sure you overlap the edges of the sleeve frills. Let dry for 4–6 hours. **E**

Add Pocket and Detailing

1 Cut a small hole at the tip of the medium-consistency green icing piping bag. Pipe a small half-oval shape in the center of the onesie to create a pocket. Cut the same piping bag tip a little bit larger and flood in the pocket shape. **F**

2 Cut a small hole at the tip of the thick-consistency pink icing piping bag. Pipe a thin outline around the flooded area. Add an extra curve by each leg to look like a hole. Pipe small dots around the body of the onesie.

3 Add two buttons between the leg holes with green icing. **G**

■ GIVE IT A THEME! ■

Making baby shower cookies to match a specific theme? The pocket space is a great area to add a flower, a teddy bear face, a snowflake, or any other small motif that goes with the theme.

Denim Jacket Cookie

This "scratching" technique creates a distressed, textured look that takes denim cookies to the next level.

Cookie and Icing List

- 1 baked cookie, cut in a jacket shape
- Flood-consistency icing, blue
- Thick-consistency icing, blue
- Thick-consistency icing, tan

Additional Materials

- Metal scribe tool
- 3 piping bags
- Scissors

JACKET COOKIE CUTTER
Any jacket-shaped cutter will work, but the one in this project is from Bobbi's Cutters.

Outline and Flood

1 Fill each piping bag with one of the listed icing colors, and set aside.

2 Outline and flood the whole cookie with flood-consistency blue icing. Let dry completely, 10–12 hours. **A**

Scratching the Cookie

1 Using the metal scribe tool, scrape the icing in long horizontal lines across the whole cookie.

2 Still using the metal scribe tool, scrape the icing in long vertical lines across the whole cookie, creating a crisscross pattern. **B**

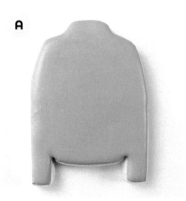

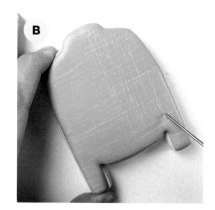

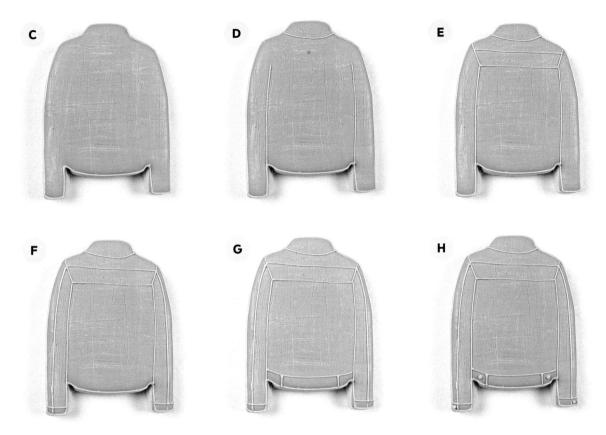

Add the Jacket Details

1. Use the thick-consistency blue icing with a small hole at the tip of the piping bag to pipe a thin outline around the full cookie. **C**

2. Add a slightly curved line connecting the collar points. Pipe two sleeve lines, starting at the bottom inner corner of each sleeve and going up to the armpit. **D**

3. Pipe a line from the shoulder angled down to the top of the sleeve line. Pipe a horizontal line connecting both sleeve lines. Pipe another line angled up to the other shoulder. Pipe an additional horizontal line through the middle of the newly formed space. **E**

4. Pipe a line from the bottom of the sleeve, closer to the outer outline, up to the angled line. Repeat on the other sleeve. Add two additional horizontal lines near the bottom of each sleeve to make the cuffs. **F**

5. Add a horizontal line near the base of the jacket body. Then add two small vertical lines near the edges of the jacket body down to the bottom of the cookie. **G**

6. Using thick-consistency tan icing with a small hole at the tip of the piping bag, add four dots to create jacket buttons, one on each cuff, and one on each side of the bottom of the jacket body. **H**

■ ADD SOME PIZZAZZ! ■

There are endless ways to jazz up a denim jacket cookie. Write "Bride" on the back for a future Mrs. or "Birthday Girl" for a unique gift topper. For more information about lettering with icing, see Lettering (page 56). For an even cuter jacket, add patches by following the instructions in Royal Icing Transfer Fireplace Cookie (page 121)!

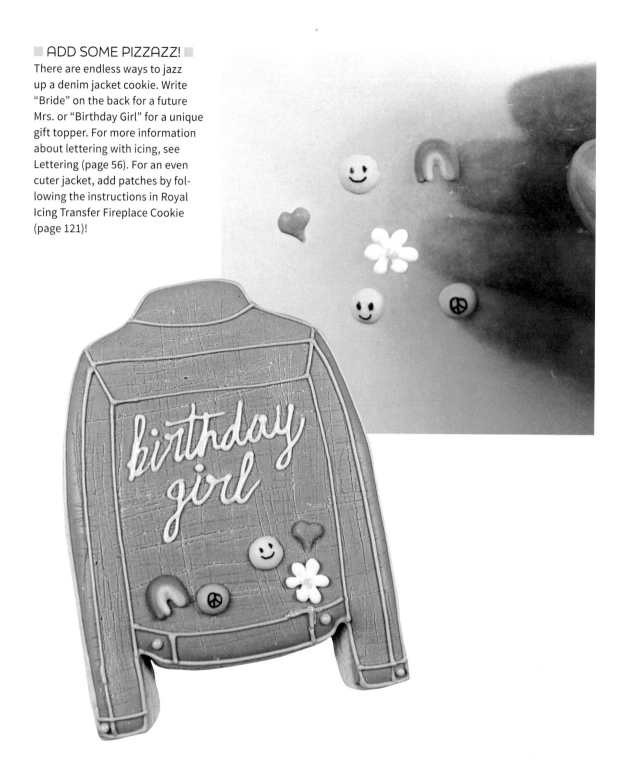

Umbrella with Raindrops Cookie

Using palette knives to shape icing results in a dimensional and unique appearance that's sure to wow.

Cookie and Icing List

- 1 baked cookie, cut in an arch shape
- Flood-consistency icing, dark blue
- Thick-consistency icing, light blue
- Thick-consistency icing, white
- Thick-consistency icing, yellow

Additional Materials

- 4 piping bags
- Palette knife
- Scissors

ARCH COOKIE CUTTER

Any arch-shaped cutter will work, but the one in this project is from KaleidaCuts.

TYPES OF PALETTE KNIVES

Palette knives come in many shapes and are made of many materials. Different shapes of knife tips will give you different results. Play around with icing on a sheet of wax paper to decide which you like best! I use a rounded knife for the umbrella and a pointed one for the raindrops.

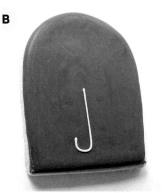

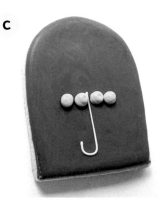

Outline and Flood

1 Fill each piping bag with one of the listed icing colors, and set aside.

2 Outline and flood the whole cookie with flood-consistency dark blue icing. Let dry completely, 12–14 hours. **A**

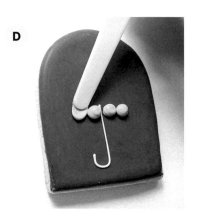

Create the Umbrella

1 Using the thick-consistency white icing with a medium-size hole at the tip of the piping bag, pipe the umbrella handle on the lower half of the cookie. **B**

2 Cut a large hole at the tip of the thick-consistency yellow icing piping bag. Pipe four large icing dots horizontally across the middle of the cookie, aligning with the top of the handle. **C**

3 Press down in the center of an icing dot with the palette knife, and drag upward, swiveling inward to the top of the umbrella and forming a rounded shape. Repeat with each icing dot, pressing down, dragging, and connecting up to the top of the umbrella. You can add more yellow icing dots and continue adjusting the shape with the dragging technique until you're happy with the curve. **D**

4 Pipe a small line at the top of the umbrella with the thick-consistency white icing. **E**

F

G

Add the Raindrops

1 Cut a medium-size hole at the tip of the thick-consistency light blue icing piping bag. Pipe icing dots for raindrops. Pipe only one or two at a time so the icing doesn't dry out before you can drag it. **F**

2 Press down in the center of each icing dot with the palette knife, and drag into a point toward the top of the cookie. Use less pressure toward the end of the point. **G H**

H

■ TURN IT UPSIDE DOWN ■

Try turning the cookie upside down when you drag the raindrops—it's more natural to drag toward yourself than away!

This chapter will introduce ways to use gel food color other than just mixing them into icing. I'll also cover color scraping, a technique that can be applied to countless cookie designs.

Jack-o'-Lantern Cookie

Color scraping adds a dimensional look to layered cookie designs and is an alternative to outlining and flooding an additional layer. Try this jack-o'-lantern design with a yellow color scrape instead of black for a candle-like glow.

Cookie and Icing List

- 1 baked cookie, cut in a pumpkin shape
- Thick-consistency icing, black
- Flood-consistency icing, orange
- Medium-consistency icing, brown
- Medium-consistency icing, green
- Thick-consistency icing, orange

Additional Materials

- Silicone Scraper tool
- 5 piping bags
- Scissors

PUMPKIN COOKIE CUTTER
Any pumpkin-shaped cutter will work, but the one in this project is from LILIAO.

Scrape the Black Icing

1   Fill each piping bag with one of the listed icing colors, and set aside.

2   Drizzle the thick-consistency black icing, from a piping bag with a medium-size hole at the tip, on the pumpkin, making sure to cover the area where a jack-o'-lantern face will go. **A**

3   Hold the cookie steady with one hand, and hold the Silicone Scraper tool at a 45° angle with the other hand. Start at the bottom of the drizzled icing, and scrape up with enough pressure to smooth the icing out. Repeat this action until you're happy with the smoothness. Let dry until set, 2–3 hours. **B**

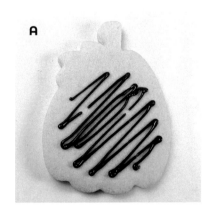

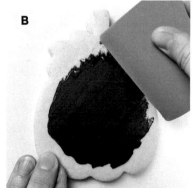

C

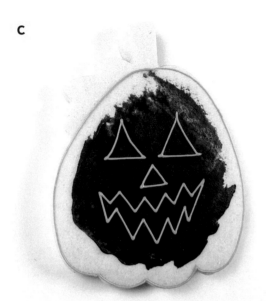

D

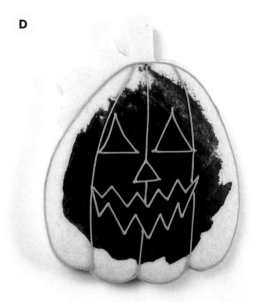

Outline and Flood the Pumpkin

1 Use the flood-consistency orange icing with a small hole at the tip of the piping bag to pipe a jack-o'-lantern face in the black area. Outline the outside of the pumpkin. **C**

2 Outline the interior sections of the pumpkin, using the cookie's shape to guide where the sections fall. **D**

3 Cut a slightly larger hole in the same piping bag, and flood alternating sections, working carefully around the face lines. Let dry until set, 2–3 hours. **E**

4 Flood the remaining sections. Let dry for another 2–3 hours.

E

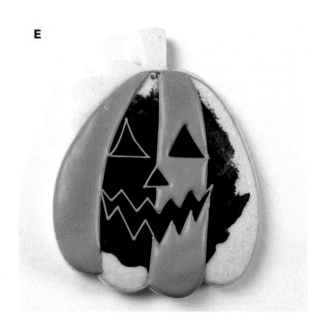

F

G

Add Details

1 Outline and flood the stem with the medium-consistency brown icing. **F**

2 Cut a small hole in the thick-consistency orange icing piping bag, and pipe lines down the pumpkin, making sure to stop and restart a line when you come to a face feature.

3 Pipe dots to look like pumpkin warts. **G**

4 Cut a small hole at the tip of the medium-consistency green icing piping bag, and pipe a line as a leaf stem. Pipe round leaves that connect to the stem. **H**

H

Taco Cookie

Give a taco shell a realistic appearance with a color splatter, which is created by mixing gel food color with water.

Cookie and Icing List

- 1 baked cookie, cut in a taco shape
- Flood-consistency icing, tan
- Thick-consistency icing, brown
- Thick-consistency icing, green
- Thick-consistency icing, red
- Thick-consistency icing, yellow
- Thick-consistency icing, white

Additional Materials

- Medium-size paintbrush
- Gel food color, brown
- Small mixing bowl
- Water
- 6 piping bags

TACO COOKIE CUTTER
Any taco-shaped cutter will work, but the one in this project is from Frosted.

Outline and Flood

1. Fill each piping bag with one of the listed icing colors, and set aside.
2. Outline and flood the taco shell using the flood-consistency tan icing, leaving room at the top of the cookie for the toppings. Let dry, 10–12 hours. **A**

Splatter the Food Color

1. Mix equal parts brown gel food color and water in the small mixing bowl using the paintbrush.
2. Dip the paintbrush in the food color mix, and hold it 6″ to 8″ above the cookie. With your other hand, tap the paintbrush to splatter the food color mix onto the cookie. **B**

PRACTICE SPLATTER SHEET
Before you splatter the food color mix onto your cookie, consider practicing on a paper towel to get the feel for the technique!

A

B

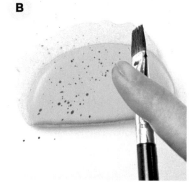

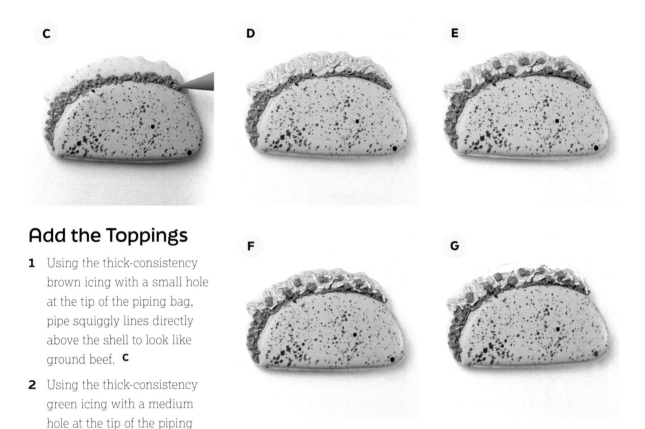

Add the Toppings

1 Using the thick-consistency brown icing with a small hole at the tip of the piping bag, pipe squiggly lines directly above the shell to look like ground beef. **C**

2 Using the thick-consistency green icing with a medium hole at the tip of the piping bag, pipe thick wavy leaf shapes above the brown icing to look like lettuce. **D**

3 Using the thick-consistency red icing with a small hole at the tip of the piping bag, pipe small squares on the green icing to look like tomatoes. **E**

4 Using the thick-consistency yellow icing with a small hole at the tip of the piping bag, pipe short thin lines to look like cheese. **F**

5 Using the thick-consistency white icing with a medium hole at the tip of the piping bag, pipe one long blob along the top of the toppings to look like sour cream. **G**

Watercolor Orange Cookie

Watercoloring gives a soft and charming feel to a cookie design. Create this effect by mixing a little bit of gel food color with water and painting it on a flooded and dried cookie.

Cookie and Icing List

- 1 baked cookie, cut in an orange shape
- Flood-consistency icing, light orange
- Flood-consistency icing, light green

Additional Materials

- Medium-size paintbrush
- Fine-detail paintbrush
- Edible ink pen
- Gel food color, orange
- Gel food color, green
- Small mixing bowl
- Plate or palette
- Water
- 2 piping bags
- Scissors

> **ORANGE COOKIE CUTTER**
> Any orange-shaped cutter will work, but the one in this project is from KaleidaCuts.

Outline and Flood

1 Fill each piping bag with one of the listed icing colors, and set aside.

2 Outline and flood the round orange area using the flood-consistency light orange icing. Let dry completely, 10–12 hours. **A**

Paint the Orange

1 Squeeze a small amount of orange gel food color onto a paint palette or plate. Fill a small bowl with water. **B**

2 Dip the medium-size paintbrush into the gel and then into the water. Mix it together on the palette or plate to see how saturated it is. Add more gel or water to your paintbrush accordingly.

A

B

3 Paint the orange in curved brushstrokes, going around the edges of the circle. Use more saturated color for the outer edges of the orange. Keep the inner area lighter by using more water on the paintbrush. Let dry, 1–2 hours. **C D**

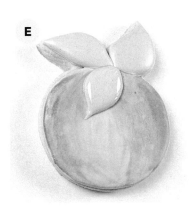

Outline and Flood the Leaves

1 Outline and flood the leaves above and on top of the orange using the flood-consistency light green icing. Be sure you allow any adjacent leaves to crust over before flooding the next leaf so the icing doesn't run together. Let leaves dry completely, 10–12 hours. **E**

Paint the Leaves

1 Squeeze a small amount of green gel food color onto a paint palette or plate. Fill a small bowl with water.

2 Dip the fine-detail paintbrush into the gel and then into the water. Mix it together on the palette or plate to see how saturated it is. Add more gel or water to your paintbrush accordingly.

3 Paint the green in curved brushstrokes, going around the edges of each leaf. Use more saturated color for the outer edges of each leaf. Keep the inner area lighter by using more water on the paintbrush. **F**

4 Using more gel than water, paint a thin line down the middle of each leaf. Paint leaf veins on half of each leaf. Let dry, 1–2 hours. **G**

Add the Face

1 Draw two curved eyes, a smile, and little dots for cheeks using the fine-point edible ink pen. **H**

One of the great things about royal icing is its ability to be layered. Since it dries hard, it can hold additional layers of icing, resulting in endless inspiration for intricate designs.

Sunshine Cookie

This sunshine design is a cheerful and detailed design full of simple layers; it's sure to brighten anyone's day.

Cookie and Icing List

- 1 baked cookie, cut in a sunshine shape
- Flood-consistency icing, light yellow
- Flood-consistency icing, mustard
- Medium-consistency icing, orange
- Medium-consistency icing, yellow
- Medium-consistency icing, black
- Thick-consistency icing, light orange
- Thick-consistency icing, white

Additional Materials

- 7 piping bags
- Scissors

SUNSHINE COOKIE CUTTER
Any sunshine-shaped cutter will work, as will a simple circle, but the one in this project is from Wella Cookie Cutter Co.

Outline and Flood

1 Fill each piping bag with one of the listed icing colors, and set aside.

2 Outline and flood the cookie using the flood-consistency light yellow icing. Let dry for 10–12 hours. **A**

Add the Center and Rays

1 Cut a small hole at the tip of the piping bag with flood-consistency mustard icing, and outline a circle in the center of the cookie, making sure to leave plenty of room from the edge for sun rays. Cut a slightly larger hole in the same piping bag, and flood the circle. **B**

A

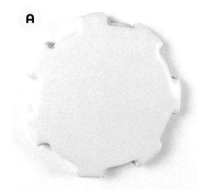

B

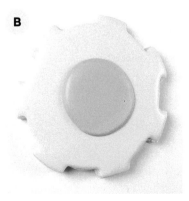

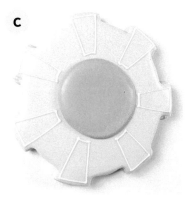

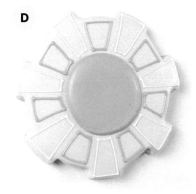

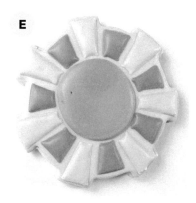

2 Cut small holes at the tips of the piping bags with the medium-consistency orange and yellow icing, and outline alternating quadrilateral shapes around the center circle, aligning with the shape of the cookie. **C D**

3 Cut medium holes at the tips of the piping bags with the medium-consistency orange and yellow icing, and flood the shapes accordingly. Let the center and rays dry for 4–5 hours. **E**

Add the Finer Details

1 Cut a small hole at the tip of the piping bag with the medium-consistency black icing, and pipe sunglasses on the center of the sun, leaving the lenses empty while the frames dry. Pipe a smile underneath.

2 Cut a small hole at the tip of the thick-consistency light orange icing piping bag. While the sunglasses dry, pipe three lines of varying lengths on each orange ray. **F**

3 Cut a small hole at the tip of the thick-consistency white icing piping bag. Pipe three lines of varying lengths on each yellow ray.

4 Flood the sunglass lenses using the medium-consistency black icing. While the black icing is still wet, pipe two diagonal glare lines in each lens using the thick-consistency white icing. **G**

Bookshelf Cookie

This layered bookshelf design can be easily customized—try different-colored books, a different number of shelves, or work in personal details and knickknacks.

Cookie and Icing List

- 1 baked cookie, cut in a large rectangle shape
- Flood-consistency icing, brown
- Medium-consistency icing, brown
- Medium-consistency icing, emerald green
- Medium-consistency icing, mauve
- Medium-consistency icing, blue
- Medium-consistency icing, light green
- Medium-consistency icing, white
- Thick-consistency icing, green

Additional Materials

- Edible ink pen
- 8 piping bags
- Scissors

Outline and Flood

1 Fill each piping bag with one of the listed icing colors, and set aside.

2 Outline and flood the cookie using the flood-consistency brown icing. Let dry for 10–12 hours.

A

Add the Shelves

1 Cut a small hole at the tip of the piping bag with the medium-consistency brown icing, and outline the whole cookie. Pipe another outline just inside the border outline.

2 Pipe four horizontal lines where the shelves will be. Pipe another horizontal line just underneath each of the existing four. **B**

3 Pipe two vertical lines down the whole cookie, dividing the cookie into even thirds. Pipe another two vertical lines just to the right of the existing two. **C**

4 Cut a slightly larger hole in the same piping bag, and flood the outlines. Let dry for 4–5 hours. **D**

Add the Books

1 Cut a small hole at the tip of the piping bag with the medium-consistency emerald-green icing, and pipe small rectangles in each shelf space to look like the spines of books. Leave space for other colored books, bookends, flower pots, and knickknacks. Allow each color to set for about 30 minutes before adding an adjacent book in a new color. **E**

> **VARIATION IS KEY**
> For a realistic look, pipe some books taller and some shorter, some wider and some thinner. Try leaving some gaps or stacking some books in a pile horizontally. Even pipe some angled books as if they've tipped over!

2 Pipe more books on the shelf space using the medium-consistency mauve icing. **F**

3 Pipe more books on the shelf space using the medium-consistency blue icing. **G**

4 Pipe more books on the shelf space using the medium-consistency light green icing. **H**

5 Pipe bookends, flower pots, vases, or knickknacks on the remaining shelf space using the medium-consistency white icing. **I**

6 Pipe leaves on top of any flower pots or vases using the thick-consistency green icing. **J**

Add Details

1 Using the edible ink pen, draw details on some of the books, such as scribbled-in titles or shapes and patterns on the spines. **K**

Koi Pond Cookie

Using a few techniques, you can produce a lifelike bird's-eye view of a koi pond.

Cookie and Icing List

- 1 baked cookie, cut in a pond shape
- Flood-consistency icing, light blue
- Flood-consistency icing, pale blue
- Medium-consistency icing, orange
- Medium-consistency icing, white
- Medium-consistency icing, red-orange
- Medium-consistency icing, green
- Thick-consistency icing, tan
- Thick-consistency icing, light gray
- Thick-consistency icing, medium gray

Additional Materials

- 9 piping bags
- Scissors

Outline and Flood

1 Fill each piping bag with one of the listed icing colors, and set aside.

2 Outline and flood the whole cookie using the flood-consistency light blue icing.

3 Use the pale-blue icing in a piping bag with a small hole at the tip to pipe curves around the pond's shape while the light blue icing is still wet. Drag the ends of the pale blue into finer lines to create a water effect. Let dry for 10–12 hours.

A

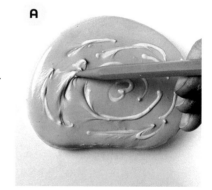

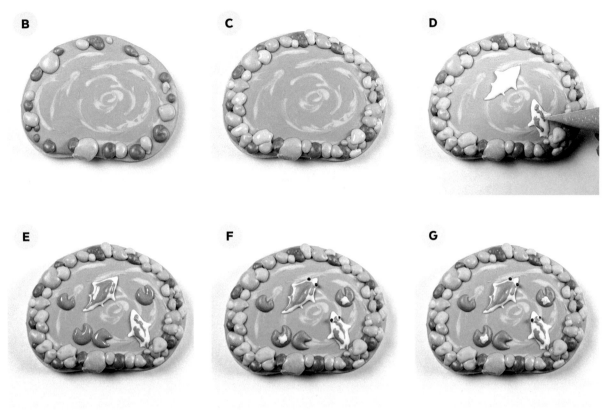

Pipe the Rocks

1 Cut medium-size holes at the tips of the thick-consistency tan, light gray, and medium gray icing piping bags. Pipe irregular blobs of icing around the border of the cookie to look like rocks using each of the three colors. Vary the sizes, shapes, and color patterns for a more organic look. Be sure each rock has crusted over before piping a neighboring one. **B C**

Pipe the Fish and Lily Pads

1 Cut a small hole at the tip of the piping bag with the medium-consistency white icing, and pipe two fish shapes on the water.

2 Cut small holes at the tips of the piping bags with the orange and red-orange icing, and pipe spots on top of the white to give the fish typical koi coloring while the white icing is still wet. **D**

3 Cut small holes at the tips of the piping bags with the medium-consistency green icing, and pipe circles with wedges left out to look like lily pads. **E**

Add the Final Details

1 Cut a small hole at the tip of the piping bag with the medium-consistency white icing, and pipe small eyes on either side of each fish's head and flowers on some of the lily pads.

2 Cut a small hole at the tip of the piping bag with the black icing, and add tiny dots to the fish eyes while the white icing is still wet. **F**

3 When the lily pad flowers have crusted over, add small detailing to the center of the flowers using a piping bag with a small hole containing the thick-consistency yellow icing. **G**

House Cookie

Part of this house design involves leaving the cookie blank through the windows—remember that the cookie can be a layer as well!

Cookie and Icing List

- 1 baked cookie, cut in a house shape
- Flood-consistency icing, pink
- Flood-consistency icing, orange-red
- Thick-consistency icing, black
- Thick-consistency icing, pink
- Thick-consistency icing, orange-red

Additional Materials

- 5 piping bags
- Scissors

> **HOUSE COOKIE CUTTER**
> Any house-shaped cutter will work, but the one in this project is from Sweetleigh Printed.

Outline and Flood the Body of the House

1 Fill each piping bag with one of the listed icing colors, and set aside.

2 Cut a small hole at the tip of the piping bag with the flood-consistency pink icing, and outline the house, excluding the roof. Outline spaces for a door and windows as well. Don't forget the chimney! **A**

3 Cut a small hole at the tip of the piping bag with the thick-consistency black icing, and pipe a thin vertical- and horizontal-line cross in each window space. **B**

A

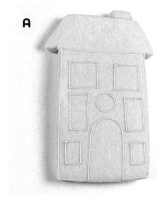

B

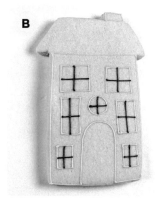

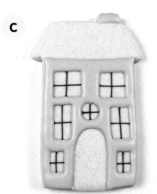

C

D

E

4 Cut a slightly larger hole in the flood-consistency pink icing piping bag. Flood the cookie, and let dry completely, 10–12 hours. **C**

Outline and Flood the Roof and Door

F

G

1 Cut a small hole at the tip of the piping bag with the flood-consistency orange-red icing, and outline the roof and the door. Cut a slightly larger hole in the same piping bag. Flood and let dry 2–3 hours until set. **D**

Add the Details

1 While the orange-red icing is drying, pipe frames around each window using the thick-consistency black icing in a piping bag with a small hole. **E**

2 Pipe thin horizontal lines on the house and thin brick-pattern details on the chimney using the thick-consistency pink icing in a piping bag with a small hole. **F**

3 When the roof and door icing has set, pipe thin scalloped lines across the roof and shapes to look like door panels on the door using the thick-consistency orange-red icing in a piping bag cut with a small hole. Add a door outline. **G**

Floral and greenery cookies are a lovely fit for lots of occasions: wedding showers, garden parties, birthdays. The list goes on and on! Even just adding a small leafy detail to a cookie design can make a big difference. This chapter will demonstrate three main leaf styles as well as a way to create lovely and detailed flowers without needing special piping tips!

Greenery Cookie

There are three main greenery styles that can be applied to all sorts of cookie designs. In this example, we'll layer all three for a full and luscious look! These are our leaf styles:

- Large single leaves
- Vine-style leaves with long wavy leaves branching out from the stem
- Pressure-piped leaf style, in which the end of the leaf farthest from the stem is largest, getting thinner as it attaches to the stem

Cookie and Icing List

- 1 baked cookie, cut in a plaque shape
- Flood-consistency icing, tan
- Thick-consistency icing, bright green
- Medium-consistency icing, sage green
- Thick-consistency icing, deep green

Additional Materials

- Edible ink pen (optional)
- 4 piping bags
- Scissors

Outline and Flood

1 Fill each piping bag with one of the listed icing colors, and set aside.

2 Outline and flood the cookie using the flood-consistency tan icing. Let dry completely, 10–12 hours. **A**

Add the Leaves

1 Cut a small hole at the tip of the piping bag with the medium-consistency sage-green icing, and pipe single, large leaves on both the top and bottom of the cookie. I pipe them to look like elongated, irregular tear-drop shapes by starting at one end, piping a curved line into a point at the tip of the leaf, and curving back to connect with the starting point. Let dry for about 30 minutes. **B**

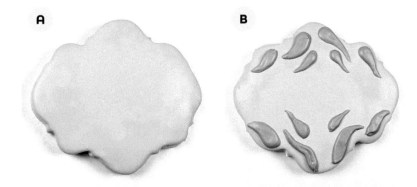

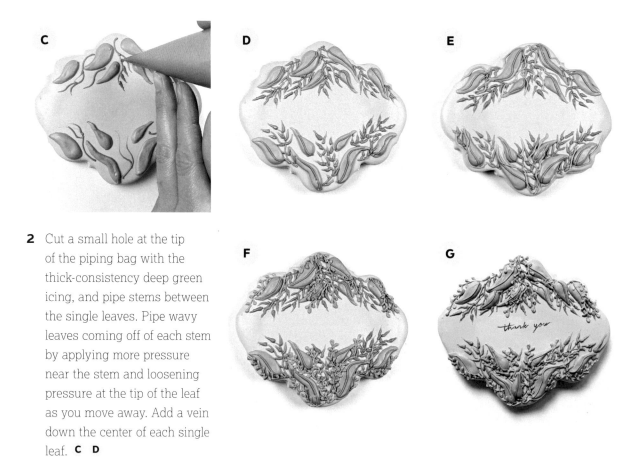

2 Cut a small hole at the tip of the piping bag with the thick-consistency deep green icing, and pipe stems between the single leaves. Pipe wavy leaves coming off of each stem by applying more pressure near the stem and loosening pressure at the tip of the leaf as you move away. Add a vein down the center of each single leaf. **C D**

3 For the third style of leaf, use the piping bag with thick-consistency bright green icing with a small hole at the tip to pipe thin stems on top of the other leaves. **E**

4 Starting away from the stem, pipe a dot of icing, and drag it to connect with the stem, forming a small, bulbous leaf. Repeat on all the bright green stems. **F**

Write a Message

1 Write a personal message or text in the center area with a fine-point edible ink pen. **G**

Floral Cluster Cookie

This flower-power cookie design demonstrates a few flower styles that can be kept simple and minimal or made more detailed with layering royal icing or edible ink markers.

Cookie and Icing List

- 1 baked cookie, cut in a circle
- Flood-consistency icing, pale blue
- Medium-consistency icing, pink
- Medium-consistency icing, purple
- Medium-consistency icing, red
- Medium-consistency icing, green
- Thick-consistency icing, green
- Thick-consistency icing, white

Additional Materials

- Edible ink markers, pink, red, and black
- 7 piping bags
- Scissors

Outline and Flood

1   Fill each piping bag with one of the listed icing colors, and set aside.

2   Outline and flood the cookie using the flood-consistency pale blue icing. Let dry completely, 10–12 hours.
A

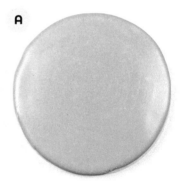
A

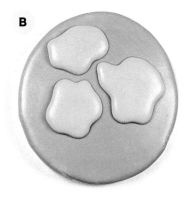

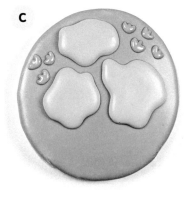

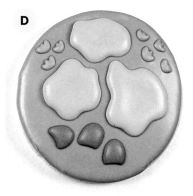

Add the Flower Shapes

1   Cut a medium hole at the tip of the piping bag with the medium-consistency pink icing, and pipe three large, abstract, and organic-shaped blobs of icing for the three main flowers. **B**

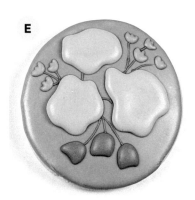

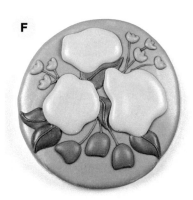

2   Cut a small hole at the tip of the piping bag with the medium-consistency purple icing, and pipe two groupings of smaller half-circle shapes with ruffles on top of each. **C**

3   Cut a medium hole at the tip of the piping bag with the medium-consistency red icing, and pipe a grouping of three medium-size half-oval shapes. Let the flower shapes dry 4–5 hours. **D**

Add the Leaf Shapes

1   Cut a small hole at the tip of the piping bag with the medium-consistency green icing, and pipe thin lines to look like stems connecting the flowers and coming toward the center of the cookie. **E**

2   Outline and flood large leaf shapes between the flowers using the medium-consistency green icing. Let the leaves dry before flooding adjacent leaves.

3   Cut a small hole at the tip of the piping bag with the thick-consistency green icing, and pipe a thin line down the center of each leaf. **F**

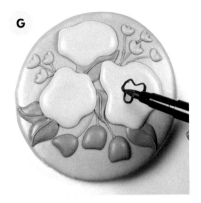

G

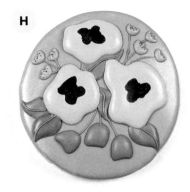

H

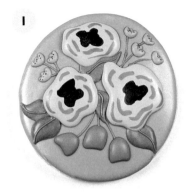

I

Add the Final Details

1 Once fully dried, draw abstract wavy shapes in the center of each pink flower using the black edible ink marker. **G**

2 Draw tiny dots near the top of each purple flower using the fine-point edible black ink pen. **H**

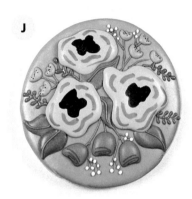

J

K

3 Draw curved lines to fit the shape of the large pink flowers with a pink edible ink marker. **I**

4 Pipe thin lines in any remaining large spaces using the thick-consistency green icing. Add leaves to some flowers with the same green icing and dots of thick-consistency white icing to others. Draw spirals and lines on the tips of the red roses with a red edible ink marker. **J**

5 Pipe white dots in the black centers of the pink flowers. **K**

Some techniques give such specific looks that they aren't used commonly. So when you do think of a perfect design to go with any of these unusual techniques, they really stand out!

Bumpy Alligator Cookie

Bubble Wrap gives flooded icing a bumpy, almost scaly texture. It also requires a bit longer drying time than normal—the material of the Bubble Wrap holds the moisture in longer!

Cookie and Icing List
- 1 baked cookie, cut in an alligator shape
- Flood-consistency icing, green

Additional Materials
- Bubble Wrap
- Edible ink markers, black and green
- 1 piping bag
- Scissors

ALLIGATOR COOKIE CUTTER
Any alligator-shaped cutter will work, but the one in this project is from Firefly Cookie Company.

Prepare the Bubble Wrap

1   Cut a section of Bubble Wrap that will cover the back area of the alligator.

Outline and Flood

1   Fill the piping bag with the icing, and set aside.

2   Outline the cookie, making sure to differentiate separate sections for the back legs, using the flood-consistency green icing. **A**

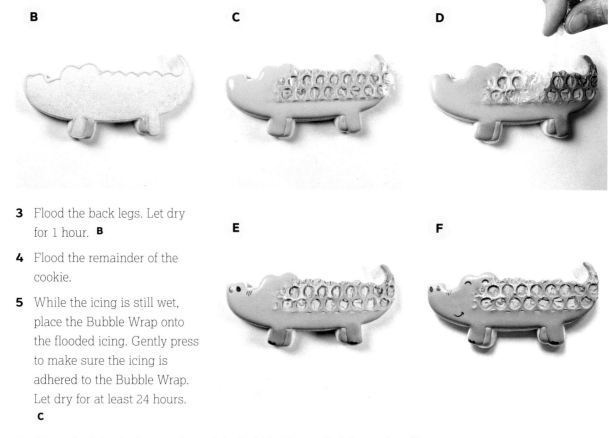

B

C

D

E

F

3 Flood the back legs. Let dry for 1 hour. **B**

4 Flood the remainder of the cookie.

5 While the icing is still wet, place the Bubble Wrap onto the flooded icing. Gently press to make sure the icing is adhered to the Bubble Wrap. Let dry for at least 24 hours. **C**

6 When the icing is dry, gently peel the Bubble Wrap off of the cookie. **D**

Add the Details

1 Draw two small circles on the alligator's snout and curved lines to look like creases using the green edible ink marker. Draw small round foot details. **E**

2 Draw two curved eyes and a curved smile using the black edible ink pen. **F**

Geode Cookie

A show-stopping geode effect can be achieved with just a little bit of clear rock candy, gel food color, and gold luster dust. Try applying this effect to all sorts of cookie shapes!

Cookie and Icing List

- 1 baked cookie, cut in a circle
- Flood-consistency icing, purple
- Flood-consistency icing, white

Additional Materials

- Small-size paintbrush
- Luster dust, gold
- Lemon extract
- Small mixing bowl
- Water
- Plate or palette
- Clear rock candy, crushed
- Gel food color, purple
- 2 piping bags
- Scissors

Outline and Flood

1 Fill each piping bag with one of the listed icing colors, and set aside.

2 Outline an organic shape where you want the geode portion to be, using the flood-consistency white icing. **A**

3 Outline and flood the remainder of the cookie using the flood-consistency purple icing. **B**

A

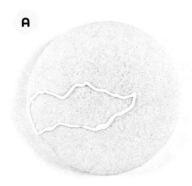

B

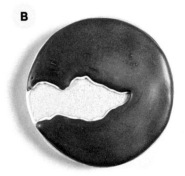

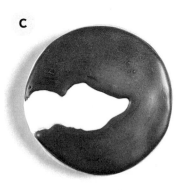

C

D

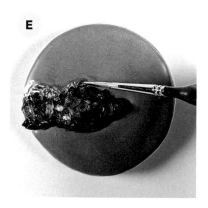

E

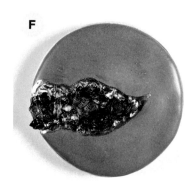

F

Fill the Geode Section

1 Flood the geode section using the flood-consistency white icing. **C**

2 While the icing is still wet, sprinkle the crushed rock candy on it, pressing gently to set the candy into the icing. Let dry for 6–7 hours. **D**

▨ CRUSHING THE ROCK CANDY ▨
To crush the rock candy as fine as you'd like it, put the rock candy in a plastic bag. Using a cutting board underneath the bag and a towel on top of the bag, crush the candy using a mallet or rolling pin.

Paint the Geode Section

1 Fill a small mixing bowl with water. Add a small amount of purple gel food color to a plate or paint palette.

2 Mix the water and the gel color with the small paintbrush, and paint the rock candy. Keep the edges more saturated and the middle less saturated. Let dry for 1–2 hours.

Add the Gold

1 Clean the small-size paintbrush. Then use it to mix equal parts lemon extract and gold luster dust in a small mixing bowl.

2 Paint the edges of the geode section gold, partly on the rock candy and partly on the purple icing surrounding the geode section. **E F**

Rustic Strawberry Patch Cookie

The unique part of this technique doesn't actually have anything to do with icing! In fact, this rustic, crackled effect is done before the dough is even baked. Brush white gel food color on a cut-out dough shape before it goes in the oven—the cookie will spread just enough for the coloring to come apart and appear crackly!

Cookie and Icing List

- Prepared dough, cut in a branch shape
- Medium-consistency icing, green
- Medium-consistency icing, red
- Thick-consistency icing, yellow
- Thick-consistency icing, green

Additional Materials

- Medium-size paintbrush
- Gel food color, white
- 4 piping bags
- Scissors

STRAWBERRY COOKIE CUTTER
Any plaque- or solid-shaped cutter will work, but the one in this project is from Little Sister Cookie.

Paint and Bake

1 Place the cut-out dough shape on the cookie sheet. Use the paintbrush to brush a thin, even layer of white gel food color across the dough shape. Bake as instructed in Cookie Dough (page 10). **A**
B

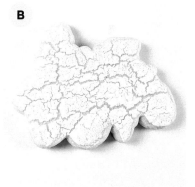

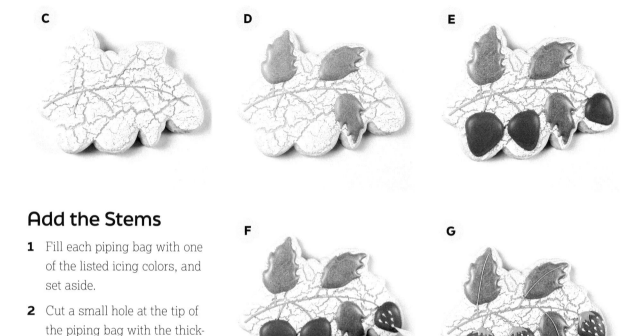

Add the Stems

1 Fill each piping bag with one of the listed icing colors, and set aside.

2 Cut a small hole at the tip of the piping bag with the thick-consistency green icing, and pipe a thin, long central stem across the cookie, followed by shorter stems branching off of it. **C**

3 Decide which stems will have strawberries and which will have leaves. Outline and flood jagged leaf shapes on the leaf stems using the medium-consistency green icing. **D**

4 Outline and flood plump, rounded triangular shapes on the dedicated strawberry stems using the medium-consistency red icing. Let leaves and strawberries dry for 10–12 hours. **E**

Add the Details

1 Cut a small hole at the tip of the piping bag with the thick-consistency yellow icing, and pipe small seeds on the strawberries. Put pressure on the piping bag as you touch the tip to the strawberry, then reduce pressure and drag down into a point. **F**

2 Pipe a line through the center of each leaf using the thick-consistency green icing. Pipe a leaf topper on each strawberry by piping a zigzag line that curves up smoothly across the top of the strawberry. **G**

Copper Mug Cookie

Sometimes you have to know the rules in order to break them, like we'll do with this hammered technique. More often than not, touching a cookie with "crusted over" icing would be a no-no. But with this technique, denting the icing as it's partially hardened forms a hammered appearance.

Cookie and Icing List

- 1 baked cookie, cut in a rounded mug shape
- Flood-consistency icing, red-orange
- Medium-consistency icing, red-orange

Additional Materials

- Medium paintbrush
- Luster dust, gold
- Lemon extract
- Small mixing bowl
- 2 piping bags
- Scissors

COPPER MUG COOKIE CUTTER
Any rounded mug–shaped cutter will work, but this one is hand-cut! See page 9 for tips about hand cutting cookie shapes.

Outline and Flood

1 Fill each piping bag with one of the listed icing colors, and set aside.

2 Outline the cup, handle, and top sections using the flood-consistency red-orange icing. **A**

A

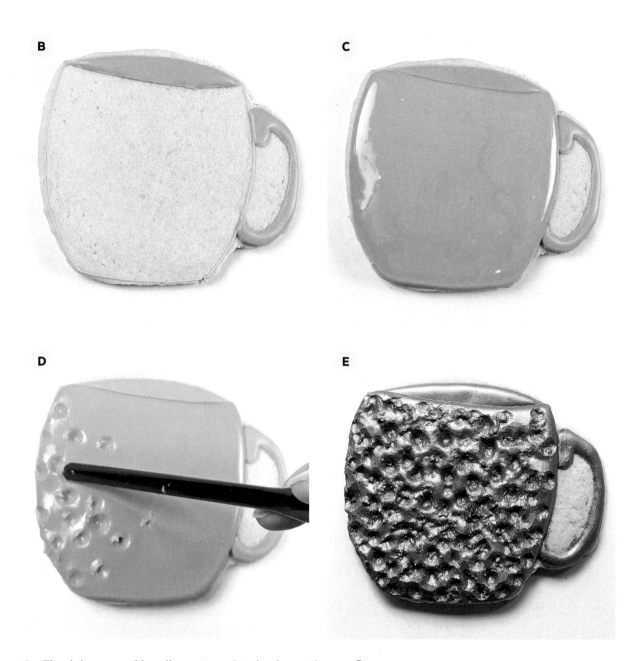

3 Flood the top and handle sections. Let dry for 1–2 hours. **B**

4 Flood the remainder of the cup. **C**

5 Let the icing dry for 30–40 minutes, until the outside appears hardened but the icing is still wet underneath. Use the back end of the paintbrush to dent the icing repeatedly to create a hammered texture. Then let it dry fully, 10–12 hours. **D**

Paint the Gold

1 Using the paintbrush, mix equal parts gold luster dust and lemon extract in the small mixing bowl. Brush the gold mixture over all the icing. **E**

Mossy Bunny Cookie

Although this technique involves baking an extra cookie, it's well worth it for the decorative mossy effect!

Cookie and Icing List

- 1 baked cookie, cut in a bunny shape
- 1 baked cookie, cut in any shape
- Flood-consistency icing, green

Additional Materials

- Food processor
- Gel food color, green
- Plate
- 1 piping bag
- Scissors

BUNNY COOKIE CUTTER
Any bunny-shaped cutter will work, but the one in this project is from Sugar Rex.

Prepare the Moss

1 Add the extra baked cookie (cut in any shape) and 4–5 drops of green gel food color to the food processor. **A**

2 Chop until the cookie is fully crumbled and green. Empty onto a plate. **B**

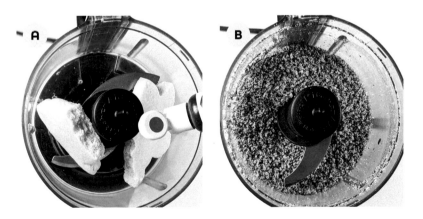

C

D

Outline, Flood, and Apply Moss to the Bunny

1   Fill the piping bag with the green icing.

2   Using the flood-consistency green icing, outline and flood the bunny cookie. **C**

3   While the icing is still wet, tap the cookie, icing side down, onto the mossy crumbs until it's fully coated. Let dry for 10–12 hours. **D** **E**

E

Sassy Sunglasses Cookie

This "stencil scrape" technique results in intricate patterns without all the intricate piping. In this example, we even get edible glitter involved. Can I get a "yes please"?

Cookie and Icing List

- 1 baked cookie, cut in a sunglasses shape
- Thick-consistency icing, black
- Medium-consistency icing, purple

Additional Materials

- Stencil
- Silicone Scraper tool
- Edible glitter spray
- 2 piping bags
- Scissors

SUNGLASSES COOKIE CUTTER

Don't have a sunglasses-shaped cutter? Try using a round, scalloped, or even heart-shaped cutter. Cut out two of each and connect with a small piece of dough. Then bake as directed in Cookie Dough (page 10).

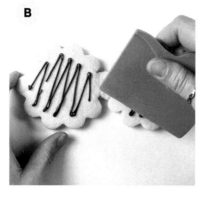

Scrape the Icing

1. Fill each piping bag with one of the listed icing colors, and set aside.

2. Using the piping bag with the thick-consistency black icing, with a medium-size hole at the tip, drizzle icing on the cookie where each lens will be. **A**

3. Steadying the cookie with one hand, hold the Silicone Scraper tool with the other hand at an angle, and drag it firmly across the cookie. Repeat on the other lens section. Let dry for 4–5 hours. **B C**

4. Place the stencil over one lens section. Drizzle the thick-consistency black icing over the existing black icing. **D**

5. Firmly drag the Silicone Scraper tool over the stencil, scraping a few times if needed, until there's an even coverage of icing. Do not lift the stencil up. **E**

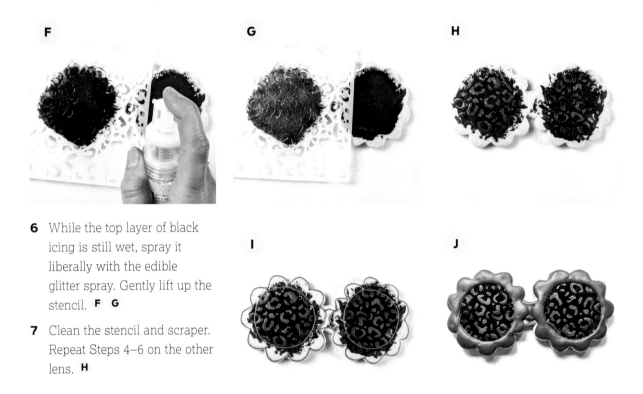

6 While the top layer of black icing is still wet, spray it liberally with the edible glitter spray. Gently lift up the stencil. **F G**

7 Clean the stencil and scraper. Repeat Steps 4–6 on the other lens. **H**

Outline and Flood the Frame

1 Using the medium-consistency purple icing, outline the cookie, including a nose piece in the center of the cookie and the two inner circles where the frames meet the lenses. **I**

2 Flood the nose piece. Let dry for 1–2 hours.

3 Flood the remainder of the frame. **J**

Ice Cream Cone Cookie

Have you ever wondered how sprinkles are made? Well guess what—they're just royal icing! This cookie will demonstrate how to make your own rainbow sprinkles (and an ice cream cone cookie design to go with, of course). Try making shaped sprinkles as well, like dots, stars, or hearts.

Cookie and Icing List

- 1 baked cookie, cut in an ice cream cone shape
- Flood-consistency icing, tan
- Thick-consistency icing, tan
- Medium-consistency icing, pink
- Medium-consistency icing, brown
- Thick-consistency icing, red
- Thick-consistency icing, yellow
- Thick-consistency icing, blue
- Thick-consistency icing, green
- Thick-consistency icing, purple

Additional Materials

- Wax paper
- Tape
- 9 piping bags
- Scissors

ICE CREAM CONE COOKIE CUTTER
Any ice cream cone–shaped cutter will work, but the one in this project is from Ann Clark Cookie Cutters.

Pipe the Sprinkles

1   Fill each piping bag with one of the listed icing colors, and set aside.

2   Tape the corners of the wax paper to a flat surface so the sheet lays smoothly.

3   Pipe thin lines across the wax paper using the thick-consistency red, yellow, blue, green, and purple icings. Let dry for 10–12 hours.

A

4 Once the icing is completely dry, peel the tape off the wax paper. Carefully bend the wax paper to break up the icing lines into smaller pieces until you have a sprinkle size you're happy with. **B** **C**

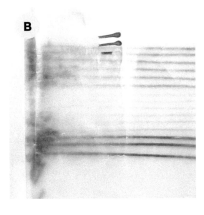

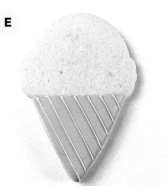

Outline, Flood, and Detail the Cone

1 Using the flood-consistency tan icing, outline and flood the cone section of the cookie. Let dry until set, 3–4 hours. **D**

2 Cut a small hole at the tip of the piping bag with the thick-consistency tan icing, and pipe diagonal lines across the cone. **E**

3 Pipe diagonal lines going the other direction, crossing over the existing lines. Let dry for 2–3 hours. **F**

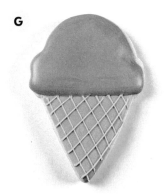

G

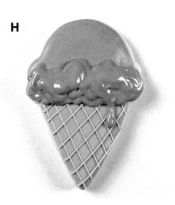

H

I

Outline, Flood, and Detail the Ice Cream

1 Outline and flood the ice cream scoop section of the cookie using the medium-consistency pink icing. Let dry until set, 3–4 hours. **G**

2 Cut a large hole at the tip of the piping bag with the medium-consistency pink icing, and pipe a thick layer on the lower portion of the scoop, above the cone. Swirl the piping bag as you pipe to give it an organic ice cream look. Agitate the icing with the Scribe Scraper tool as it begins to dry to prevent it from getting too smooth. Pipe a drip going down the cone. Allow to dry for 10–12 hours. **H**

J

Add the Hot Fudge and Sprinkles

1 Using the piping bag with the medium-consistency brown icing cut with a medium-size hole, outline and flood the top portion of the ice cream scoop, creating drips going down the scoop.

2 While the icing is still wet, carefully drop the sprinkles onto the icing. **I** **J**

Royal Icing Transfer Fireplace Cookie

Royal icing transfers are icing designs that have been piped onto wax paper, dried, and then peeled off. Think of them as custom sprinkles! One benefit of these is that they offer more forgiveness than piping directly onto a particularly detailed cookie design. They also offer a lot of control with placement and give a lovely 3D effect.

Cookie and Icing List

- 1 baked cookie, cut in a fireplace shape
- Thick-consistency icing, black
- Flood-consistency icing, red-brown
- Medium-consistency icing, white
- Medium-consistency icing, dark brown
- Medium-consistency icing, red
- Medium-consistency icing, orange
- Medium-consistency icing, yellow

Additional Materials

- Edible ink pen, brown
- Silicone Scraper tool
- Sheet of cardstock paper
- 7 piping bags
- Sheet of wax paper
- Tape
- Scissors

FIREPLACE COOKIE CUTTER
Any fireplace-shaped cutter will work, as will a simple square or rectangle, but the oversized cutter in this project is from Butter Cutters.

Scan this QR code or visit tinyurl.com/11552-patterns-download to access a downloadable practice PDF that includes a sheet of the shapes used for the royal icing stocking transfers in this project.

Prepare the Transfer Sheet

1 Using the QR code above, download and print the provided sheet of stocking images.

2 Set the wax paper on top of the stocking drawings. Tape the corners of the wax paper to a flat surface so the sheet stays in place. **A**

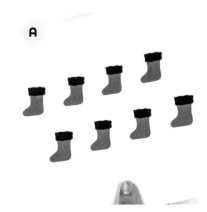

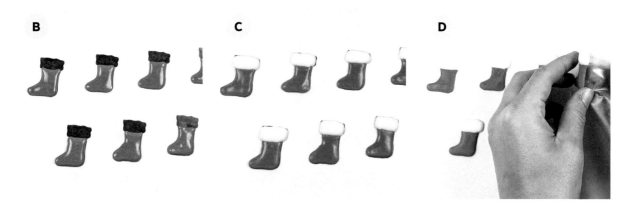

Pipe the Transfers

1 Fill each piping bag with one of the listed icing colors, and set aside.

2 Cut a medium-size hole at the tip of the piping bag with the medium-consistency red icing, and pipe on top of the wax paper to match the stocking design. Let dry for 1–2 hours. **B**

3 Cut a medium-size hole at the tip of the piping bag with the medium-consistency white icing, and pipe the white areas of the stockings on top of the wax paper. **C**

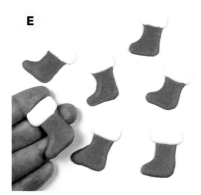

> ▪ TRANSFERS TIP! ▪
> It's a good idea to pipe more royal icing transfers than you need in case of breakage!

4 Let the transfers dry completely, 10–12 hours.

5 When the transfers are dried, carefully peel them off the wax paper. **D E**

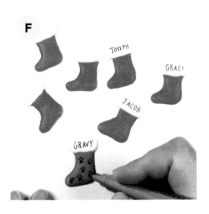

6 Add personalized edible ink pen details to the transfers, if desired. **F**

Scrape, Outline, and Flood

1 Cut a medium-size hole at the tip of the piping bag with the thick-consistency black icing, and drizzle the icing in the center-bottom of the cookie, making sure to cover the area that will be the inside of the fireplace. Hold the cookie steady with one hand, and hold the Silicone Scraper tool at a 45° angle with the other hand. Start at the bottom of the drizzled icing, and scrape up with enough pressure to smooth the icing out. Repeat this action until you're happy with the smoothness. Let dry for 1–2 hours. **G**

2 Outline and flood the main part of the fireplace using the flood-consistency red-brown icing. Let dry for 10–12 hours. **H**

Add the Fireplace Details

1 Draw horizontal lines across the red-orange icing to achieve the look of bricks, using the brown edible ink pen.

2 Draw short vertical lines across each row, offsetting the lines from the row above. **I**

Add the Mantel

1 Outline and flood the mantel and the hearth at the top and bottom of the cookie using the medium-consistency dark brown icing. Let dry for 2–3 hours. **J**

2 Outline and flood an additional layer on the top and bottom rectangles of the mantel and hearth to add dimension. **K**

N

O

P

Pipe the Fire

1 Cut a medium hole at the tip of the piping bag with the medium-consistency yellow icing, and pipe a flame shape within the black section of the fireplace.

2 While the icing is still wet, pipe the medium-consistency orange and red icings into the yellow. Use a Scribe Scraper tool to form into flame-like points. **L**

Add Wood Detailing to the Mantel

1 Add organic wood lines to the top mantel section using the brown edible ink pen. **M**

Apply the Transfers

1 Pipe a small amount of medium-consistency white icing to the back of a royal icing stocking, and adhere it below the mantel. Repeat for the remaining transfers. **N** - **P**

Cookie Sets

When creating a set of cookies, you'll likely want a few designs that match a theme. Think about what designs make sense together. Variety can be great: Maybe one cookie has text, one is image based, and one is patterned. How will the colors coordinate? Will all the cookies be the same shape, or will they vary? Do you want similar textures or a variety?

The fun thing about making a set of cookies is that there are no right or wrong answers to these questions. Let your creativity take over!

While decorating a set of cookies, it's important to think ahead and coordinate the timing of each design as much as possible. For example, rather than doing one cookie design from start to finish and then starting the next cookie design, it's a good idea to flood all the designs together so they can dry at the same time. Then apply the next level of details at the same time, and so on and so forth. This way, you'll complete each of the cookie designs more or less around the same time!

BRIDAL BEAUTY SET

Whether for an engagement party, a bridal shower, a bachelorette party, a rehearsal dinner, or the wedding itself, a bridal-themed set is a staple! This set includes a wedding dress, a ring, and a cake. Customize the cake style or the background stencil-scrape pattern on the ring cookie to fit the right wedding vibe!

Cookie and Icing List

- 1 baked cookie, cut in a cake-on-a-stand shape
- 1 baked cookie, cut in a ring shape
- 1 baked cookie, cut in a dress shape
- Flood-consistency icing, white
- Flood-consistency icing, tan
- Medium-consistency icing, tan
- Thick-consistency icing, white
- Thick-consistency icing, green

Additional Materials

- Silicone Scraper tool
- Small mixing bowl
- Luster dust, gold
- Lemon extract
- Flat-edge paintbrush
- Decorative stencil
- Fine-detail paintbrush
- 5 piping bags
- Scissors

COOKIE CUTTERS

The ring-shaped cutter and the dress-shaped cutter in this project are from Ann Clark Cookie Cutters. The cake-shaped cutter in this project is from KaleidaCuts.

Outline and Flood

1 Fill each piping bag with one of the listed icing colors, and set aside.

2 Outline and flood the cake section of the cake cookie, excluding the cake stand, using the flood-consistency tan icing. **A**

3 Outline the whole ring cookie using the flood-consistency white icing. Flood the ring cookie. **B**

4 Outline the top of the dress cookie. Separate the sections of the bottom of the dress using the flood-consistency white icing. **C**

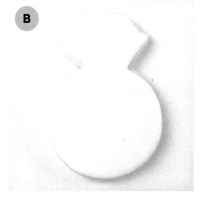

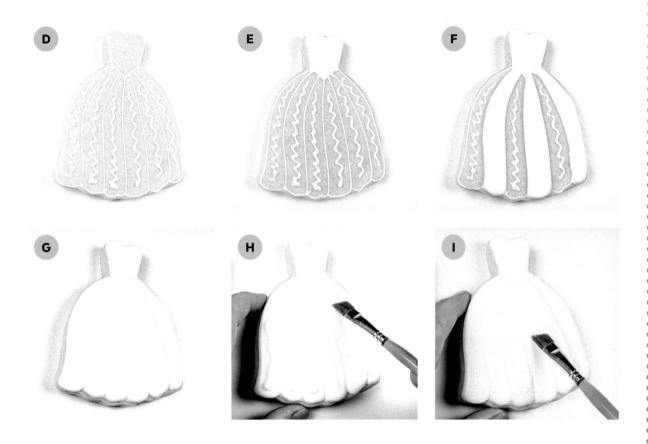

5 Drizzle flood-consistency white icing in each dress section to give it a fuller look after it's flooded. **D**

6 Flood the top of the dress cookie. **E**

7 Flood alternating sections of the dress, letting them set before flooding adjacent sections. Let all cookies dry for 10–12 hours. **F** **G**

Add the Details to the Dress Cookie

1 Drizzle icing on each portion of the dress cookie, excluding the top, using the thick-consistency white icing.

2 Brush the icing down each section using the flat-edge paintbrush to create a chiffon look. **H** **I**

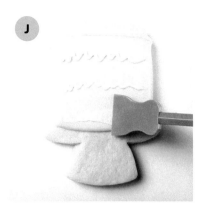

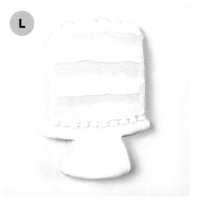

Add the Details to the Cake Cookie

1 Drizzle three horizontal lines across the cake cookie using thick-consistency white icing. Using the scraper end of the Scribe Scraper tool, scrape the icing horizontally to spread it partially across the cake. Continue layering and scraping icing until it's as thick or thin as you'd like it. **J**

2 Outline and flood the cake stand using the flood-consistency white icing. Let dry for 1 hour. **K**

3 Cut a medium-size hole at the tip of the piping bag with the thick-consistency white icing, and pipe detailing at the bottom of the cake by starting at one end, piping a dot, and dragging it into a point. Pipe another dot overlapping with the first one, and drag into a point. Continue until the bottom of the cake has been covered.

4 Pipe larger dots of icing at the top of the cake using the thick-consistency white icing. Let dry for 30 minutes. **L**

5 Cut a small hole at the tip of the piping bag with the thick-consistency green icing, and pipe thin stems on the bottom and top of the cake, as if they are coming around the sides of the cake. Pipe small leaves on the stems. **M N**

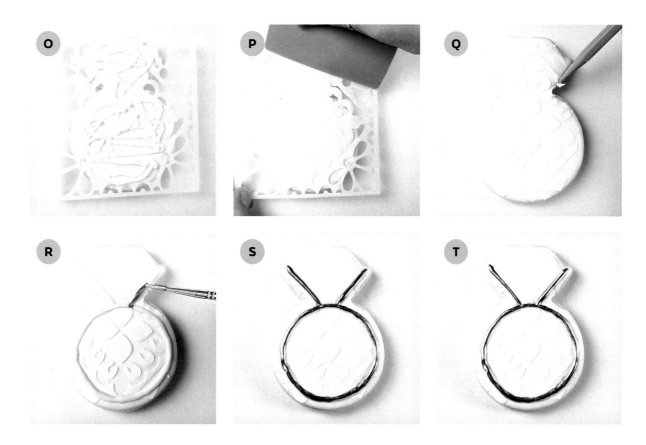

Add the Details to the Ring Cookie

1 Place the stencil over the ring cookie, and drizzle the thick-consistency white icing over the stencil. For more about using a stencil, see Sassy Sunglasses Cookie (page 115). **O**

2 Using the Silicone Scraper tool, scrape the icing fully across the cookie. Gently lift up the stencil, and clean up the edges with the scribe tool if needed. **P Q**

3 Cut a medium-size hole at the tip of the piping bag with the medium-consistency tan icing, and pipe a circle on the ring cookie. Pipe two angled lines into the diamond section. Let dry for 4–5 hours.

4 Mix equal parts gold luster dust and lemon extract in a small mixing bowl using a fine-detail paintbrush.

5 Brush the tan icing with the gold. **R**

6 Outline and flood a diamond shape on the ring using the flood-consistency white icing. Let dry until set. **S**

7 Using the piping bag with the thick-consistency white icing with a small hole at the tip, pipe a thin horizontal line across the farthest points of the diamond. Pipe a *W* shape above the horizontal line. Pipe a *V* shape below the horizontal line, reaching the bottom. **T**

HELLO BABY SET

Baby cookies are about as sweet as it gets—literally! There are endless ways to customize these baby carriage, rattle, and balloon arch designs. Try different text or colors!

Cookie and Icing List

- 1 baked cookie, cut in a baby carriage shape
- 1 baked cookie, cut in a rattle shape
- 1 baked cookie, cut in an arch shape
- Flood-consistency icing, white
- Flood-consistency icing, tan
- Flood-consistency icing, sage green
- Medium-consistency icing, white
- Medium-consistency icing, tan
- Medium-consistency icing, sage green
- Thick-consistency icing, white
- Thick-consistency icing, tan
- Thick-consistency icing, sage green

Additional Materials

- 9 piping bags
- Scissors

COOKIE CUTTERS

The arch-shaped cutter in this project is from KaleidaCuts. The rattle-shaped cutter in this project is from Jameson Cookie Company. The baby carriage–shaped cutter in this project is from Sugar Rex.

Outline and Flood

1 Fill each piping bag with one of the listed icing colors, and set aside.

2 Outline and flood the arch cookie and baby carriage cookie using the flood-consistency white icing. **A B**

3 Outline and flood the top circle section and the bottom handle section of the rattle cookie using the flood-consistency sage green icing. Let all three cookies dry for 10–12 hours. **C**

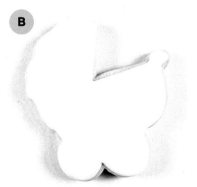
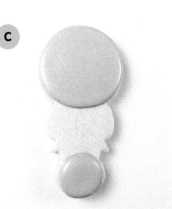

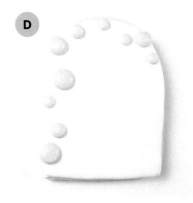

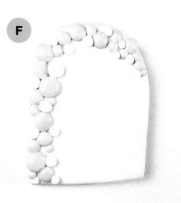

Add the Details to the Balloon Arch Cookie

1 Using the piping bag with the medium-consistency tan icing with a medium-size hole at the tip, pipe dots in a variety of sizes along the left edge of the arch cookie, spacing them out from the bottom of the cookie to just past the curve. Let them set before piping any dots that touch each other. **D**

2 Repeat Step 1 with the medium-consistency sage green icing. **E**

3 Repeat Step 1 with the medium-consistency white icing. **F**

4 Add more icing dots to fill in any space until you're pleased with the fullness of the balloon arch. **G**

5 Using small, thin-script text, pipe *hello baby* along the base using the thick-consistency sage green icing. For more about piping lettering and thin script, see Lettering (page 56). **H**

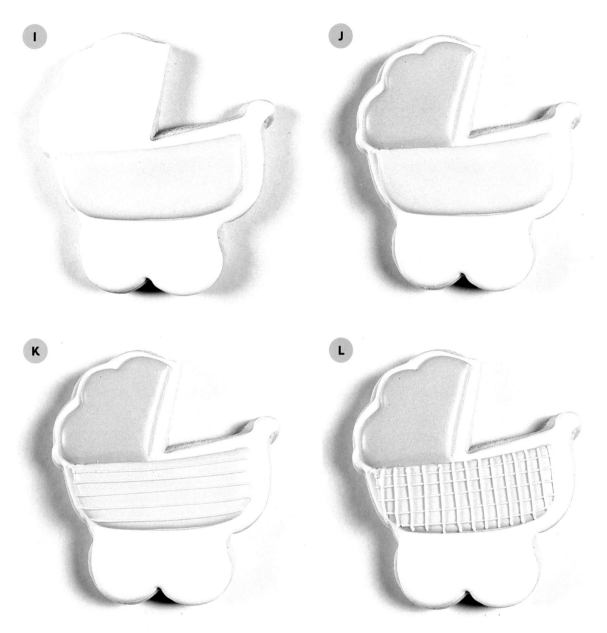

Add the Details to the Baby Carriage Cookie

1 Outline and flood the body of the carriage in a half-oval shape using the flood-consistency tan icing. Let dry for 4–5 hours. **I**

2 Outline and flood the cover of the carriage using the flood-consistency sage green icing by piping three scallops on the left side and, angling downward, following the shape of the cookie to meet the carriage body. Let dry for 2–3 hours. **J**

3 Using the piping bag with the thick-consistency tan icing with a small hole at the tip, pipe thin repeating parallel horizontal lines across the body of the carriage. For more about piping details, see Fine-Line Piping (page 38). **K**

4 Pipe thin repeating parallel vertical lines down the body of the carriage. **L**

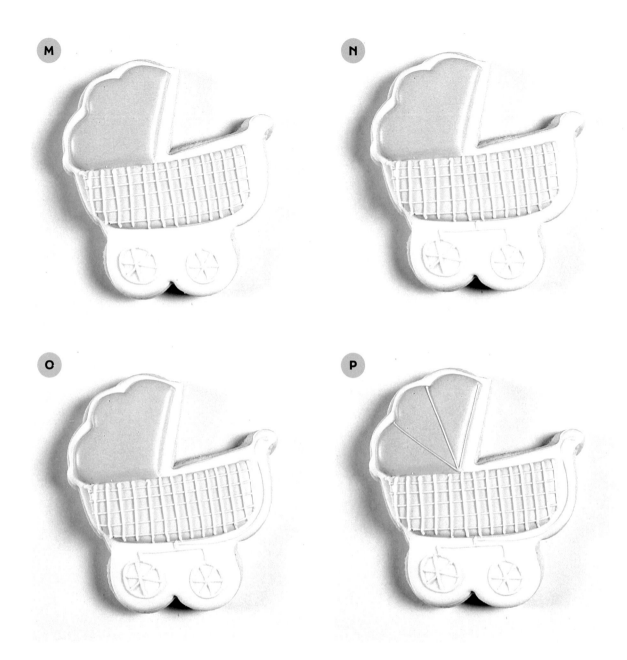

5 Pipe two circles for the wheels, followed by three straight intersecting lines in each circle. **M**

6 Pipe straight lines connecting the base of the carriage to the wheels. **N**

7 Pipe the handle of the carriage by piping a curved line from the middle base of the carriage body up to the top right of the cookie. **O**

8 Using the thick-consistency sage green icing, pipe three lines, one from each point of the scallops down to the bottom right corner of the carriage cover. **P**

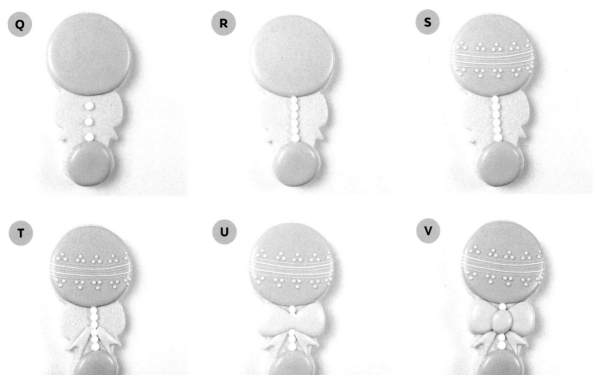

Add the Details to the Rattle Cookie

1 Pipe three dots of medium-consistency white icing in a vertical line along the rattle handle, leaving even spacing between each. Let them dry for 30–60 minutes. **Q**

2 Fill in the space between the dots with additional dots to complete the handle. **R**

3 Using the piping bags with the thick-consistency sage green and white icings with small holes at the tips, pipe decorative lines and dots on the large circle of the rattle. **S**

4 Pipe and flood an angled shape on either side of the handle to look like the tails of the bow using the medium-consistency tan icing. Let dry for 30–60 minutes. **T**

5 Pipe a bow shape across the handle. Let dry for 30–60 minutes. **U**

6 Pipe a circle in the center of the bow. Let dry for 30–60 minutes. **V**

7 Using the piping bag with the thick-consistency tan icing with a small hole at the tip, pipe a thin oval outline at the top of each side of the bow. Pipe a thin line on either side of the bow coming out from the center circle. **W**

WITCHY SET

The secret ingredient of this set? Just a little bit of magic. Using a limited color palette of black, white, and purple—with accents of silver—gives this cookie set a cohesive feel. Imagine them with green in place of purple. Or maybe gold instead of silver!

One cookie in this set uses a complex hand design. Scan this QR code or visit tinyurl.com/11552-patterns-download to access a downloadable practice PDF that includes a sheet of hand shapes to practice with. Print the designs to the desired size, lay a sheet of wax paper on top, and pipe over them for practice. When you start piping on the cookie, it helps to have the image printed near you or pulled up on your phone. For more about detailed piping, see Fine-Line Piping (page 38).

Cookie and Icing List

- 1 baked cookie, cut in a rectangle shape
- 1 baked cookie, cut in a crystal ball shape
- 1 baked cookie, cut in an arch shape
- Flood-consistency icing, white
- Flood-consistency icing, purple
- Flood-consistency icing, black
- Thick-consistency icing, white
- Thick-consistency icing, black

Additional Materials

- Scribe Scraper tool
- Small mixing bowl
- Luster dust, silver
- Lemon extract
- Flat-edge paintbrush
- 5 piping bags
- Scissors

CRYSTAL BALL COOKIE CUTTER
Any crystal ball–shaped cutter will work, but the one in this project is from Firefly Cookie Company.

Outline and Flood

1. Fill each piping bag with one of the listed icing colors, and set aside.

2. Outline and flood the rectangle cookie using the flood-consistency white icing.

3. Outline and flood the arch cookie using the flood-consistency purple icing.

4. Outline the ball section of the crystal ball, leaving the base blank for now, using the flood-consistency black icing. Flood the ball by swirling flood-consistency black and purple icings. Use the Scribe Scraper tool to swirl the icing further. Let all three cookies dry for 10–12 hours. See Wet-on-Wet Icing (page 30) for more about this flooding technique. **A**

A

Add the Silver Splatter

1. Mix even parts silver luster dust with lemon extract in the small mixing bowl using the paintbrush.

2. Dip the paintbrush in the silver mixture, hold it 6″ to 8″ above the arch and crystal ball cookies, and tap it with your finger, splattering the mixture on both cookies. **B**

B

Add the Details to the Crystal Ball Cookie

1   Using the thick-consistency white icing in a piping bag with a small hole at the tip, pipe small star shapes, sparkles, and dots at the top left region of the crystal ball. **C**

2   Outline and flood the base of the crystal ball cookie using the flood-consistency white icing. Let dry for 5–6 hours.

3   Mix more silver luster paint, and paint the base. **D**

Add the Details to the Mystic Hands Cookie

1   Cut a small hole at the tip of the piping bag with the thick-consistency white icing, and pipe the top of one hand, starting on the top left side of the arch cookie. The arched line should have subtle angles for the wrist and knuckles. Form curved bends in the finger. **E**

2   Flip the cookie upside down, and pipe the same initial hand shape from Step 1. **F**

3   Pipe the pointer and middle fingers, each bent at a different angle, on both the top and the bottom hands. **G**

4   Pipe the ring finger onto the top and bottom hands. **H**

5   Pipe a thumb, rounded palm, and the bottom line of the wrist on both the top and bottom hands. **I**

6   Pipe small star shapes, sparkles, and dots in the center of the cookie, between the hands. **J**

Add the Details to the Tarot Card Cookie

1 Using the thick-consistency black icing in a piping bag with a small hole at the tip, pipe a thin frame near the outer edges of the rectangle cookie. Pipe rounded notches at each corner. Leave more space at the bottom of the cookie than at the other three sides. **K**

2 Pipe the words *THE SUN* in the space at the bottom. **L**

3 Within the frame area, pipe a circle with two eye shapes for the head of the sun. **M**

4 Pipe thin sunbeam strokes from all sides of the circle in varying lengths. **N**

5 Pipe two small pupil circles at the top of each eye shape. **O**

6 Pipe small star shapes, sparkles, and dots to fill the remaining space inside the frame. **P**

OTHER TAROT CARDS
If you're making a whole set of witchy cookies, try making a variety of tarot cards! Use the same frame, and replace the text and imagery with other simple tarot-inspired designs.

CHRISTMAS MINIS SET

Mini cookies are a fun way to make even more cookie designs within one set. Due to their size, mini cookies tend to be decorated in less detailed ways, which gives them a cute and minimal look! Mini cookies can be a nice option to have at events where there will be many other desserts and people want just a bite of each. These will be a perfect addition to this year's Christmas dessert table!

Cookie and Icing List

- 6 baked cookies, cut in small circles, approximately 1.5″ to 2″
- Flood-consistency icing, white
- Flood-consistency icing, red
- Flood-consistency icing, brown
- Flood-consistency icing, skin tone
- Medium-consistency icing, white
- Medium-consistency icing, red
- Medium-consistency icing, orange
- Thick-consistency icing, yellow
- Medium-consistency icing, skin tone
- Medium-consistency icing, black
- Thick-consistency icing, white

Additional Materials

- 11 piping bags
- Scissors

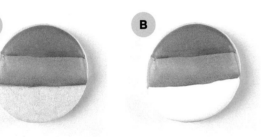

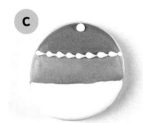

Outline and Flood

1   Fill each piping bag with one of the listed icing colors, and set aside.

2   Outline and flood two of the cookies using the flood-consistency red icing.

3   Outline and flood two of the cookies using the flood-consistency brown icing.

4   Outline and flood one of the cookies using the flood-consistency white icing.

5   Outline the top third of the remaining cookie using the flood-consistency red icing. Outline the middle third of the same cookie using the flood-consistency skin-tone icing. Flood the red and skin-tone icings, wet-against-wet. For more about the wet-against-wet technique, see Sunset Cookie (page 36). **A**

6   Let all six cookies dry for 10–12 hours.

Add the Details to the Santa Face Cookie

1   Outline and flood the remaining third of the red and skin-tone cookie using the flood-consistency white icing. **B**

2   Cut a medium-size hole at the tip of the piping bag with the thick-consistency white icing, and pipe a dotted line on the base of the red section to form the hat trim. Pipe one dot, and drag it to the right to form a point, then start the next dot on top of the point of the previous dot. Pipe a larger dot at the top of the hat. **C**

3   When the flooded white icing has set, pipe one-half of a mustache shape using the medium-consistency white icing. **D**

4   When the first mustache half has set, pipe the other half. **E**

5   Using the thick-consistency black icing in a piping bag with a small hole at the tip, pipe two dots for the eyes. **F**

6 When both parts of the mustache have set, pipe a nose directly above the mustache using the medium-consistency skin-tone icing. **G**

7 Scribble remaining hair on the sides of the face using the thick-consistency white icing. **H**

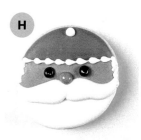

Add the Details to the Santa Belt Cookie

1 Using the medium-consistency black icing, outline and flood a thin rectangle across the center of one of the red cookies to look like a belt. Let dry for 1–2 hours. **I**

2 Using the thick-consistency white icing in a piping bag with a small hole at the tip, pipe squiggly lines back and forth to form a fuzzy rectangle perpendicular to the belt. Let dry for 1 hour. **J**

3 Using the thick-consistency yellow icing in a piping bag with a medium-size hole at the tip, pipe a square buckle in the center of the belt. **K**

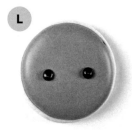

Add the Details to the Reindeer Cookie

1 Using the thick-consistency black icing in a piping bag with a small hole at the tip, pipe two eyes centered on one of the brown cookies to be the reindeer's eyes. **L**

2 Pipe two short angled lines at the top of the cookie. Add two shorter angled lines stemming from each to form antlers. **M**

3 Using the medium-consistency red icing in a piping bag with a medium-size hole at the tip, pipe a round nose centered beneath the eyes. **N**

Add the Details to the Snowman Cookie

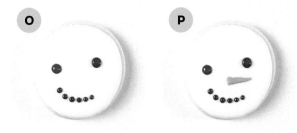

1   Using the thick-consistency black icing in a piping bag with a small hole at the tip, pipe two eyes centered on the white cookie to be the snowman's eyes.

2   Pipe smaller black dots in a curved row near the bottom of the cookie to be the smile. **O**

3   Using the thick-consistency orange icing in a piping bag with a small hole at the tip, pipe an irregular elongated triangle between the eyes and smile to look like a carrot nose. **P**

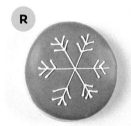

Add the Details to the Snowflake Cookie

1   Using the thick-consistency white icing in a piping bag with a small hole at the tip, pipe three intersecting lines centered on one of the red cookies. For more about piping details, see Fine-Line Piping (page 38). **Q**

2   Pipe two V shapes toward the top of each of the six lines of the snowflake. **R**

3   Pipe small dots near the middle, one between each section of the snowflake. **S**

Add the Details to the Gingerbread Man Cookie

1   Using the thick-consistency black icing, pipe two eyes and a smile on the flooded brown cookie. **T**

2   Pipe a squiggly line above the face using the thick-consistency white icing. **U**

3   Pipe two rosy cheeks using the medium-consistency red icing. **V**

When you can't keep your plants alive, make them out of dough and icing instead! Try different patterns and colors on the planters.

Cookie and Icing List

- 1 baked cookie, cut in a hanging plant shape
- 1 baked cookie, cut in a succulent shape
- 1 baked cookie, cut in a potted plant shape
- Flood-consistency icing, white
- Flood-consistency icing, brown
- Flood-consistency icing, black
- Flood-consistency icing, deep green
- Flood-consistency icing, mossy green
- Flood-consistency icing, kelly green
- Flood-consistency icing, lime-green
- Medium-consistency icing, white
- Thick-consistency icing, brown
- Thick-consistency icing, black
- Thick-consistency icing, deep green
- Thick-consistency icing, kelly green

Additional Materials

- 12 piping bags
- Scissors

COOKIE CUTTERS
The cutters in this project are from KaleidaCuts.

Outline and Flood the Planters

1 Fill each piping bag with one of the listed icing colors, and set aside.

2 Outline and flood the planter section of the hanging plant cookie using the flood-consistency white icing. **A**

3 Outline and flood the planter section of the succulent cookie using the flood-consistency black icing. **B**

4 Outline and flood the planter section of the potted plant cookie using the flood-consistency tan icing. Let all cookies dry until set, 4–5 hours. **C**

A

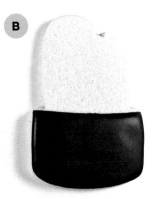

B

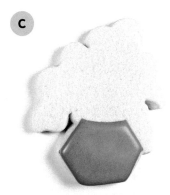

C

D

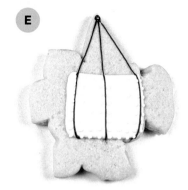

E

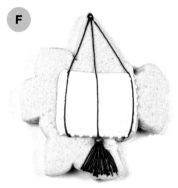

F

Add Details to the Planters

For more about piping details, see Fine-Line Piping (page 38).

G

H

1   Using the piping bag with the medium-consistency white icing with a small hole at the tip, pipe dots on the hanging planter. Let the dots dry for 30–60 minutes. **D**

2   Add the hanging strings. Using the thick-consistency black icing in a piping bag with a small hole at the tip, pipe a small circle at the top of the hanging plant cookie. Pipe a line going straight down from the circle to the bottom of the planter. Pipe another line from the circle to the right top of the planter (but not all the way to the edge) and then down the side of the planter. Pipe another line from the circle to the left top of the planter (but not all the way to the edge) and then down the side of the planter. **E**

3   Pipe thin, angled lines coming out from the bottom of the center black line below the planter to form a tassel. Continue layering the piped lines until the tassel is as full as you'd like. Pipe a dot of icing where the planter and tassel connect, using the thick-consistency brown icing. **F**

4   Pipe a pattern of thin horizontal lines and dotted lines on the succulent planter using the thick-consistency black icing. **G**

5   Using the thick-consistency tan icing in a piping bag with a small hole at the tip, pipe a thin horizontal line in the middle of the potted plant's planter. Pipe thin angled lines on both halves, following the angles of the planter. Pipe an outline of the planter and another thin horizontal line across the middle, on top of the existing one. **H**

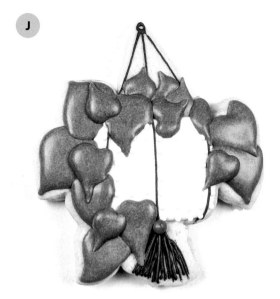

Add Leaves to the Hanging Plant

1 Using the flood-consistency deep green icing in a piping bag with a medium-size hole at the tip, pipe heart-shaped leaves around the hanging planter. Let each leaf set before piping any adjacent leaves. **I**

2 Continue piping and layering leaves until the hanging planter cookie looks full. Pipe leaves in varying sizes and directions for an organic look. **J**

3 When all leaves have set, pipe a thin line in the middle of each leaf using the thick-consistency deep green icing in a piping bag with a small hole at the tip. **K**

Add the Succulents

1 Outline two tall, rounded succulent shapes, layering so that one appears in front and the other appears behind it using the flood-consistency mossy green icing. **L**

2 Flood the back succulent, and let dry 1–2 hours. **M**

3 Flood the front succulent, and let dry 1–2 hours. **N**

CREATING DEPTH

When piping an image in which one object is visually in front of another, pipe the "in-front" object last so that the flood icing overlaps the existing flood, giving it more realistic dimension.

4 Pipe thin vertical lines on each succulent using the medium-consistency white icing in a piping bag with a small hole at the tip. **O**

5 Pipe tiny dots along each line and a flower on top of the front succulent. **P**

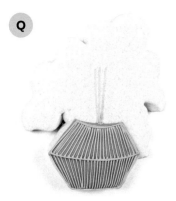

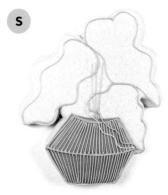

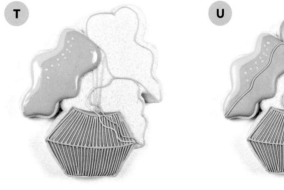

Add Leaves to the Potted Plant

1 Using the flood-consistency kelly green icing in a piping bag with a small hole at the tip, pipe three thin, vertical stems from the center top of the planter. Slightly angle the stems away from one another. Each stem should go about three-quarters of the way up the cookie. **Q**

2 Outline three large wavy leaves using the flood-consistency kelly green icing, leaving a thin space on one side of each leaf for a second flooded color. **R**

3 Pipe the outer section of each leaf using the flood-consistency lime-green icing. **S**

4 Using the wet-against-wet technique, flood the large section of one leaf with the flood-consistency kelly green icing in a piping bag with a slightly larger hole at the tip. While this section is still wet, flood the thinner section with the flood-consistency lime-green icing in a piping bag with a slightly larger hole at the tip. While this section is still wet, using the wet-on-wet technique, pipe small dots of the flood-consistency lime-green icing on the flooded kelly green icing. Let dry for 30–60 minutes before flooding the leaves that touch. For more about the wet-against-wet technique, see Sunset Cookie (page 36), and for more about the wet-on-wet technique, see Wet-on-Wet Icing (page 30). **T**

5 When all the leaves have set, pipe a thin wavy line on the center of each leaf using the medium-consistency kelly green icing. **U**

OUTER SPACE SET

This cookie set is out of this world! Okay, too predictable? Well, the techniques involved in this set won't be. Get ready for some parchment paper, luster dust, and wet-on-wet icing to make these designs come to life!

Cookie and Icing List

- 1 baked cookie, cut in an oval shape
- 1 baked cookie, cut in a rocket shape
- 1 baked cookie, cut in a tall arch shape
- Flood-consistency icing, light purple
- Flood-consistency icing, dark purple
- Flood-consistency icing, black
- Flood-consistency icing, white

- Flood-consistency icing, yellow
- Medium-consistency icing, blue
- Medium-consistency icing, green
- Medium-consistency icing, orange
- Medium-consistency icing, gray
- Medium-consistency icing, red
- Thick-consistency icing, black
- Thick-consistency icing, light purple
- Thick-consistency icing, blue
- Thick-consistency icing, dark purple

Additional Materials

- Silicone Scraper tool
- Parchment paper
- Tape
- 14 piping bags
- Scissors

ROCKET COOKIE CUTTER
Any rocket-shaped cutter will work, but the one in this project is from Ann Clark Cookie Cutters. The tall arch cutter is from Wella Cookie Cutter Co. The oval cutter is from KaleidaCuts.

Outline and Flood

1 Fill each piping bag with one of the listed icing colors, and set aside.

2 Outline the tall arch and the oval cookie using the flood-consistency black icing.

3 Flood the tall arch cookie with the black icing.

4 Flood the oval cookie with the black icing. While the icing is still wet, pipe small swirls and stars with the flood-consistency light purple and white icings in piping bags with small holes at the tips. Drag the icing with the Scribe Scraper tool to swirl further, and drag the star tips into finer points. For more about the wet-on-wet technique, see Wet-on-Wet Icing (page 30). **A**

5 Using the thick-consistency black icing in a piping bag with a medium-size hole at the tip, drizzle icing on the middle of the rocket cookie. Use the Silicone Scraper tool to scrape the icing across the center portion of the cookie where the rocket's window will go. Let dry for 20–30 minutes. For more about color scraping, see Jack-o'-Lantern Cookie (page 81). **B** **C**

6 Outline and flood the body of the rocket, including a circle in the middle for the window, using the flood-consistency purple icing. Let all three cookies dry for 10–12 hours. **D**

A

B

C

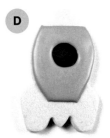
D

Add Details to the Planets Cookie

1 Cut a small hole at the tip of the piping bag with the medium-consistency blue icing, and pipe a circle to look like a planet on the oval cookie. While the icing is still wet, using the medium-consistency green icing, pipe areas of green to make it look like planet Earth. **E**

2 Cut a small hole at the tip of the piping bag with the medium-consistency orange icing, and pipe another planet on the oval cookie. **F**

3 Cut a small hole at the tip of the piping bag with the medium-consistency gray icing, and pipe a moon on the oval cookie. Let dry for 30 minutes. **G**

4 Though the icing will look dry on the top, the inside will still be wet. During this time, poke the moon repeatedly with the Scribe Scraper tool to create a cratered look. For more about icing punctures, see Copper Mug Cookie (page 111). **H**

5 Pipe a ring around the orange planet using the thick-consistency purple icing in a piping bag with a small hole at the tip. **I**

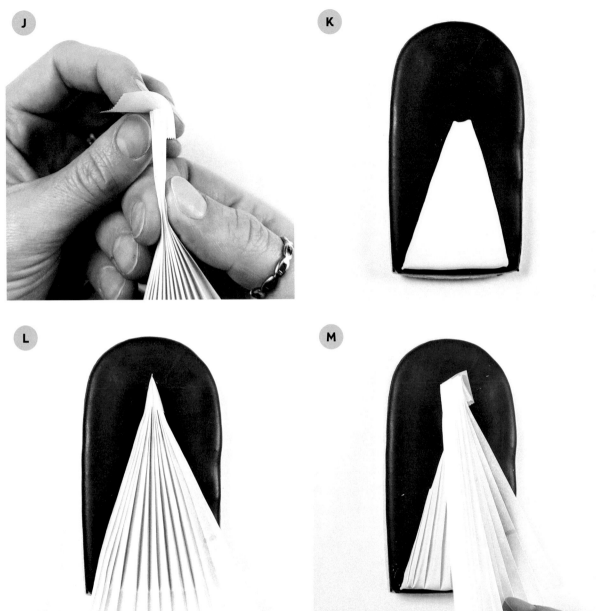

Add Details to the UFO Cookie

1   Create a parchment paper fan by folding the paper tightly back and forth. Tape the top of one end so it forms a triangular shape. For more about this parchment paper texture, see Mountain Range Cookie (page 51). **J**

2   Outline and flood a triangular-shaped beam of light on the tall arch cookie using the flood-consistency yellow icing. Be sure to leave room above the light beam for the UFO. **K**

3   While the icing is still wet, gently press the parchment paper fan onto the yellow icing. Let dry for 8–10 hours. **L**

4   Once dried, gently peel the parchment paper off the icing. **M**

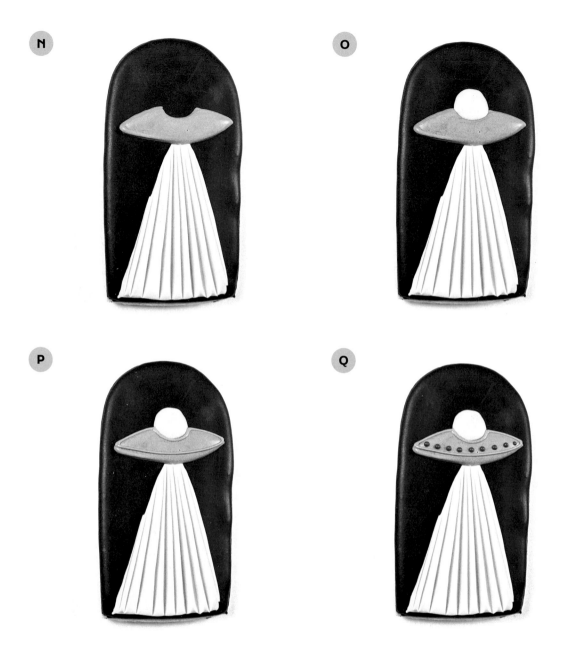

5 Outline and flood a disc shape, with the bottom touching the top of the light beam, using the flood-consistency light purple icing. Leave a half-circle blank at the top center where the cockpit will go. Let it set for 1–2 hours. **N**

6 Outline and flood a dome shape for the cockpit using the flood-consistency blue icing. While the icing is still wet, pipe a thin glare mark using the medium-consistency white icing. Let dry for 1–2 hours. **O**

7 Outline the top half of the disc shape using the thick-consistency light purple icing. **P**

8 Pipe dots above the center curved line using the thick-consistency dark purple icing in a piping bag with a small hole at the tip. **Q**

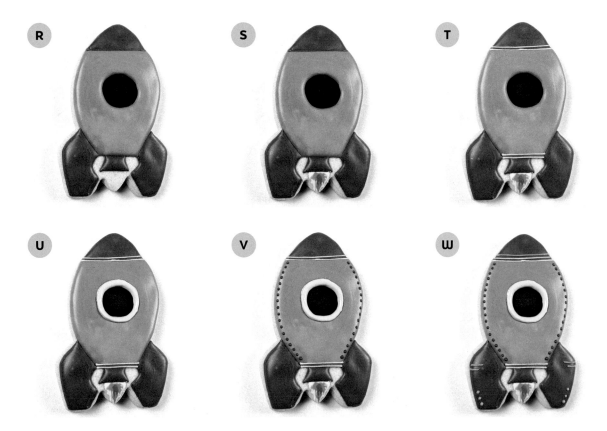

Add the Details to the Rocket Cookie

1. Outline and flood the tip, wings, and base of the rocket using the flood-consistency dark purple icing. Let dry for 1–2 hours. **R**

2. Pipe a jagged flame shape below the base of the rocket using the medium-consistency yellow icing in a piping bag with a small hole at the tip. While the icing is still wet, add the medium-consistency orange and red icings in piping bags with small holes at the tips. Use the Scribe Scraper tool to drag the icing into flame shapes. **S**

3. Pipe two thin lines across the top and bottom of the body of the rocket using the medium-consistency blue icing in a piping bag with a small hole at the tip. **T**

4. Outline and flood a circle around the window of the rocket using the medium-consistency blue icing. **U**

5. Pipe small dots along the left and right edges of the rocket's body using the thick-consistency purple icing in a piping bag with a small hole at the tip. **V**

6. Pipe thin lines and dots on the rocket's wings using the thick-consistency light purple icing in a piping bag with a small hole at the tip. **W**

PAINT-YOUR-OWN HALLOWEEN SET

Paint-your-own cookies are fun to make and fun to paint—not to mention fun to eat! This set includes cookies with piped designs and one cookie with an icing "paint palette." Grab a clean paintbrush, dip it in water, mix the palette colors, and paint away! These make great activities for kids (or adults!) at parties. Try other themes as well! For more about piping details, see Fine-Line Piping (page 38).

Cookie and Icing List

- 3 baked cookies, cut in square shapes
- 3 baked cookies, cut in small rectangle shapes
- Flood-consistency icing, white
- Medium-consistency icing, black
- Medium-consistency icing, yellow
- Medium-consistency icing, green
- Medium-consistency icing, orange
- Medium-consistency icing, purple
- Medium-consistency icing, blue
- Thick-consistency icing, black

Additional Materials

- 8 piping bags
- Scissors

Before you Bake

1 To form small rectangles for the paint palettes that are the same width as the square cookies, use the same square cookie cutter, but cut the dough again as shown to form a thinner shape. **A**

Outline and Flood

1 Fill each piping bag with one of the listed icing colors, and set aside.

2 Outline and flood each square and rectangle cookie using the flood-consistency white icing. Let dry for 10–12 hours. **B**

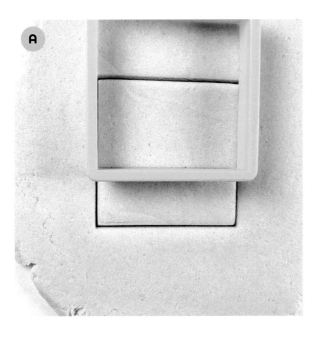

A

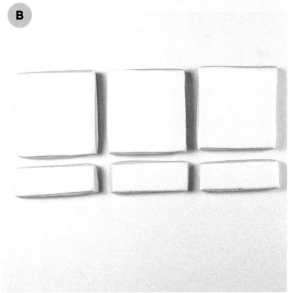

B

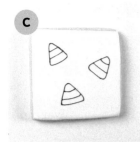 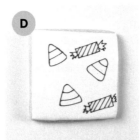  

Add the Design to the Candy Cookie

1 Using the thick-consistency black icing in a piping bag with a small hole at the tip, pipe three rounded triangles. Add two lines through each rectangle to form three candy corn shapes. **C**

2 Pipe two striped rectangles with jagged shapes at both ends to look like wrapped candies between the candy corns. **D**

3 Pipe two swirly circles with sticks as lollipops between the other candies. **E**

4 Pipe additional circles in the leftover space. **F**

Add the Design to the Jack-o'-Lantern Cookie

1 Pipe a large round pumpkin shape with a stem in the center of one of the square cookies using the thick-consistency black icing. **G**

2 Pipe a jack-o'-lantern face in the center of the pumpkin. **H**

3 Pipe curved vertical lines across the pumpkin, making sure the face spaces are left clear. **I**

4 Pipe a leaf on the stem and stars in the space around the pumpkin. **J**

Add the Design to the Haunted House Cookie

1 Pipe a slightly curved horizontal line on one of the square cookies using the thick-consistency black icing. Add a curved pathway below it. **K**

2 Pipe a funky house shape with different shaped windows and a door above the horizontal line. **L**

3 Pipe the top portion of the house and the roof. **M**

4 Continue adding sections to the house, on its sides, and coming off the roof, with more windows. Make them harshly angled for a spooky and silly look! **N**

5 Pipe a fence on either side of the house, a moon in the sky, and stones in the walkway. **O**

Add the "Paint" to the Palette Cookies

1 Cut large holes in the piping bags with the medium-consistency black, yellow, green, orange, purple, and blue icings, and pipe four evenly sized dots of icing on each of the three smaller rectangle cookies, alternating colors. Let dry. **P**

BOOKISH SET

This reading set is the perfect treat to go with that book you just can't put down. Customize the text on the bookmark or the titles on the book stack! Add the Bookshelf Cookie (page 91) to this set!

Cookie and Icing List

- 1 baked cookie, cut in a book stack shape
- 1 baked cookie, cut in a rectangle
- 1 baked cookie, cut in a thin rectangle with a hole toward the top
- Flood-consistency icing, white
- Flood-consistency icing, golden yellow
- Flood-consistency icing, light blue
- Flood-consistency icing, navy blue
- Flood-consistency icing, pink
- Medium-consistency icing, white
- Medium-consistency icing, tan
- Thick-consistency icing, white

Additional Materials

- Small mixing bowl
- Luster dust, gold
- Lemon extract
- Fine-tip paintbrush
- Fine-tip edible ink pen, black
- Fine-tip edible ink pen, blue
- Thick piece of paper
- Ribbon
- 8 piping bags
- Scissors

BOOK STACK COOKIE CUTTER
Any book stack–shaped cutter will work, but the one in this project is from Firefly Cookie Company.

Before You Bake

1 Use a straw to cut a small hole out of the rectangular cookie dough for the bookmark shape. **A**

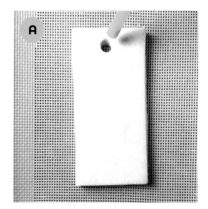

Outline and Flood

1 Fill each piping bag with one of the listed icing colors, and set aside.

2 Outline the rectangle library card cookie and the second from the bottom book on the book stack cookie using the flood-consistency golden yellow icing.

3 Outline the bookmark cookie and the bottom book on the book stack cookie using the flood-consistency navy icing.

4 Outline the top book on the book stack cookie using the flood-consistency light blue icing. Leave the second from the top book on the book stack cookie empty for now. **B**

5 Flood the library card and second from the bottom book on the book stack cookie using the flood-consistency golden yellow icing. **C**

6 Flood the bookmark cookie using the flood-consistency navy blue icing. **D**

7 Flood the top cookie on the book stack using the flood-consistency light blue icing. **E**

8 Let the library card and bookmark cookies dry for 10–12 hours. Let the book stack cookie dry 1–2 hours until set.

9 Flood the bottom book on the book stack cookie using the navy blue icing.

10 Using the flood-consistency pink icing in a piping bag with a medium-size hole at the tip, pipe two thick lines on the top and bottom of the second book from the top of the book stack cookie. Let dry for 1–2 hours. **F**

11 Flood the center of the second book from the top of the book stack cookie using the flood-consistency white icing. **G**

Add the Details to the Library Card Cookie

1 Using the thick piece of paper and the fine-point black edible ink pen, draw a horizontal line about ½″ from the top of the cookie. Draw more horizontal lines about a ¼″ apart until you reach the bottom of the cookie. **H**

2 Leaving the first two rows blank, draw three vertical lines, evenly spaced, down the cookie. **I**

3 Write *Date Due* in the top row.

4 Write *Title* in the second row. Add a book title of your choice if desired! **J**

5 Write due dates in the left column, formatted as month abbreviation, date, year.

■ MAKE IT AUTHENTIC ■

To give the due dates a more authentic stamped look, use a small piece of paper towel to smudge some of the dates directly after writing, as if the stamp smeared. You could write a few dates in blue edible ink for stamp pad variety.

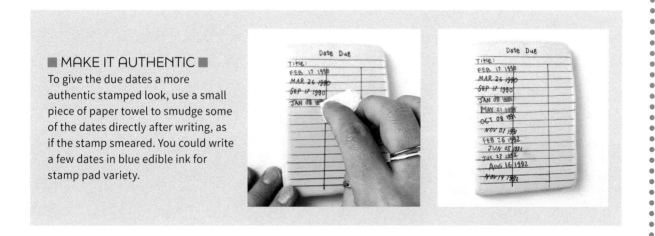

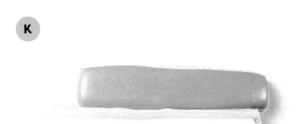

Add the Details to the Book Stack Cookie

1 Using the thick-consistency white icing in a piping bag with a small hole at the tip, pipe thin horizontal lines in the white area of the second book from the top to form pages. **K**

2 Pipe book titles of your choosing on the three books with outward-facing spines. This is a fun chance to experiment with different lettering styles! **L**

3 Pipe decorative details on the book spines such as stripes or stars on either end. **M**

Add the Details to the Bookmark Cookie

1 Using the medium-consistency white and tan icings in piping bags with small holes at the tips, pipe the words *I Read Past My Bedtime* on the bookmark cookie. Anything piped in tan icing will be brushed with a gold effect later on. Pipe the middle part of the phrase first to give yourself more control over the spacing. Start with *Past* near the middle of the cookie. For more about lettering, see Lettering (page 56). **N**

2 Pipe the word *Read* above the existing word using the medium-consistency tan icing. **O**

3 Pipe the word *My* below *Past* using the medium-consistency white icing. **P**

4 Pipe the word *Bedtime* below *My* using the medium-consistency tan icing.

5 Pipe the word *I* above *Read* using the medium-consistency white icing. **Q**

6 Pipe a crescent moon in the corner using the medium-consistency white icing.

7 Pipe stars in the remaining space using the medium-consistency tan and white icings. **R**

8 Mix equal parts gold luster dust and lemon extract in the small mixing bowl using the fine-tip paintbrush. Once the tan icing is dry, paint it with the gold paint. Add a ribbon through the hole for a real bookmark effect. **S**

CRAFTY SET

There are so many forms of art (cookie decorating included!) that it's tough to choose just a few for this crafter's set. Try a different pattern on the quilt square cookie or limited colors on the paint palette cookie!

Cookie and Icing List

- 1 baked cookie, cut in a cross-stitch hoop shape
- 1 baked cookie, cut in a paint palette shape
- 1 baked cookie, cut in a square
- Flood-consistency icing, white
- Flood-consistency icing, brown
- Flood-consistency icing, royal blue
- Flood-consistency icing, tan
- Flood-consistency icing, red
- Medium-consistency icing, red
- Medium-consistency icing, orange
- Medium-consistency icing, yellow
- Medium-consistency icing, green
- Medium-consistency icing, blue
- Medium-consistency icing, purple
- Thick-consistency icing, green
- Thick-consistency icing, white
- Thick-consistency icing, red

Additional Materials

- 6″ × 6″ parchment paper
- Luster dust, silver
- Lemon extract
- Small mixing bowl
- Small paintbrush
- Edible ink markers, various colors
- 14 piping bags
- Scissors
- Chua Cookie perforated silicone baking mat

BEFORE YOU BAKE

Don't have a cross-stitch hoop cutter? Try using a circle cutter and adding a small, short T shape of dough to the top before you bake it! Make sure you bake this batch on the Chua Cookie perforated silicone baking mat as we'll use the textured underside of the baked cookie in the design. The palette cutter in this project is from Frosted.

Outline and Flood

1. Fill each piping bag with one of the listed icing colors, and set aside.

2. Outline and flood the paint palette cookie using the flood-consistency white icing.

3. Outline and flood a ½″ circle around the underside of the cross-stitch cookie using the flood-consistency brown icing. **A**

4. While the brown icing is still wet, gently lay the parchment paper on top, adhering it to the wet icing. Allow to dry completely before peeling off. **B C**

5. Before outlining and flooding the quilt square cookie, use an edible ink marker to draw the design. **D**

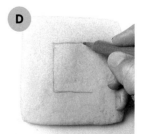

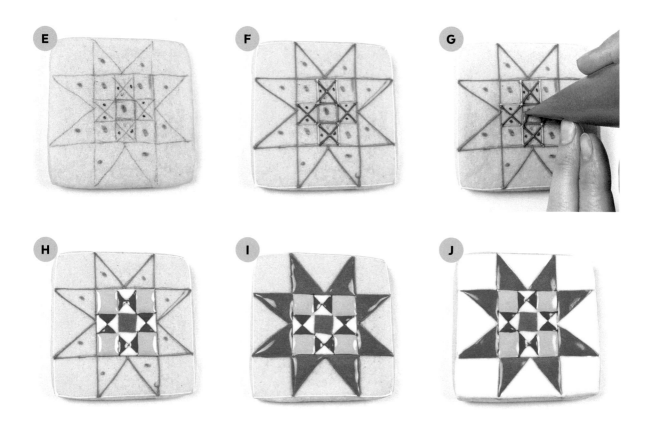

6   Use additional edible ink markers to mark which sections will be which colors. This can be helpful when using a wet-against-wet technique with multiple colors. For more about the wet-against-wet technique, see Sunset Cookie (page 36). **E**

7   Outline the marker lines with the corresponding icing colors. **F**

8   Flood the cookie wet-on-wet, starting with the innermost section and using flood-consistency red icing. Flood the next sections using flood-consistency white and royal blue icings. Flood the next sections with flood-consistency light blue icing. Flood the final outer sections with flood-consistency white and red icings. Let all cookies dry for 10–12 hours. **G** - **J**

K

L

Add the Details to the Paint Palette Cookie

1 Using the medium-consistency red, orange, yellow, green, blue, and purple icings in piping bags with medium-size holes at the tips, pipe an irregular blob shape of each color around the paint palette. K L

2 Pipe smaller blobs of each color near the larger blobs of the same color. M

M

Add the Details to the Cross-Stitch Cookie

1   Using the thick-consistency green icing in a piping bag with a very small–size hole at the tip, pipe a line of small *X* shapes to form a flower stem. **N**

2   Pipe two additional stems made up of small *X* shapes on either side of the existing stem. **O**

3   Pipe two leaf shapes, one on each outer stem, made up of small *X* shapes. **P**

4   Using the thick-consistency red icing, pipe a scalloped half circle made up of small *X* shapes at the top of the middle stem. **Q**

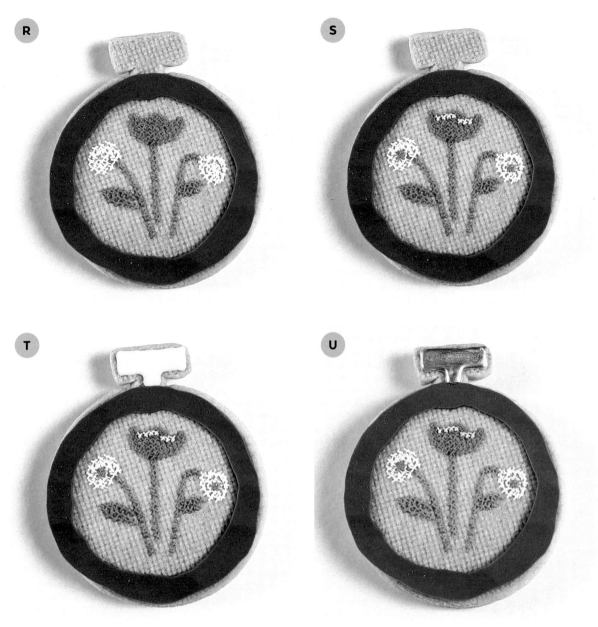

5 Using the thick-consistency white icing, pipe two circular shapes, one at the top of each outer stem, made up of small *X* shapes. **R**

6 Using the thick-consistency white icing, pipe a thin grouping of small *X* shapes toward the top of the red flower. Using the thick-consistency red icing, pipe a round grouping of small *X* shapes at the center of each white flower. **S**

7 Using the flood-consistency white icing, outline and flood the top *T* area above the hoop. Let dry 2–3 hours. **T**

8 Mix equal parts silver luster dust and lemon extract in the small mixing bowl using the paintbrush, and apply to the *T* shape at the top of the hoop. **U**

Troubleshooting

Sometimes things don't go as planned. Mistakes happen to everyone! As if errors weren't enough of a bummer, it can be frustrating to not know why something went wrong or how you can prevent it in the future. Below, some common uh-ohs, whoopsies, and what-the-hecks are explained!

Color Bleeding

What does it look like?

Color bleeding occurs when the dye from one color of icing starts to bleed into a neighboring color.

Why does it happen?

This happens when an icing color is flooded next to another icing color that isn't fully dry or set. The fresh moisture in the newly flooded icing reactivates the remaining moisture in the first color. Color bleeding is more likely to happen with highly saturated icings that contain a higher amount of dye.

How can I prevent it?

To prevent color bleeding, make sure icing colors have dried properly before applying neighboring icing colors. Also try allowing bold icing colors to saturate overnight before piping. Gel food color makes icing bolder with time, and this means less gel food color is incorporated into the icing. However, you'll still get a bright color with a little patience.

How can I work with it if it's already happened?

If a color has already started to bleed into another color, try piping details on top of the bleed area with a thick-consistency icing. It will cover the area without introducing more moisture.

Craters

What does it look like?

Craters occur when a section of icing that was intended to be "puffed," rounded, or full ends up sinking or caving in as it dries.

Why does it happen?

This can happen when a loose icing is piped in a large blob without a "scribble layer" underneath to give it more height and volume.

How can I prevent it?

Drizzle a layer of icing in the dedicated space before filling in fully with icing. In addition, put the cookie in front of a fan or in a low-heat dehydrator for 30 to 60 minutes directly after piping the detail. This will harden the icing before it has the chance to cave. I use the scribble technique on the dress cookie in the Bridal Beauty Set (page 127).

How can I work with it if it's already happened?

If it works with the design, try piping greenery or a floral design over the caved-in icing. Or you might use the scraper end of the Scribe Scraper tool to scrape away the cratered icing and try again.

Air Bubbles

What does it look like?

Air bubbles look like small dark spots, almost like freckles, on hardened icing.

Why does it happen?

Air bubbles can occur during the flooding process when pockets of air are formed as the icing comes together. If the icing dries with air bubbles, they appear as darker dots on the surface.

How can I prevent it?

To prevent air bubbles, be sure to give freshly flooded cookies a few taps on a table to bring any air bubbles up to the surface of the icing. From there, use the Scribe Scraper tool to pop the air bubbles and swirl them back into the icing smoothly. Review Outlining and Flooding (page 20).

How can I work with it if it's already happened?

Fortunately, air bubbles most commonly occur in the flood layer, which is often covered up by additional details. However, if you do have some air bubbles showing, try piping a design over them or using an edible ink pen to make a polka dot background—the air bubbles will blend right in.

Butter Bleeding

What does it look like?

Butter bleeding occurs when the oils in the cookie seep into the icing, saturating the color in dark splotchy patches.

Why does it happen?

This can happen with moist cookies and is more likely in high-humidity climates.

How can I prevent it?

Try letting the baked cookies dry just a bit before decorating them. For example, bake the night before decorating rather than flooding them as soon as they're cooled. This will allow the cookies to soak in more of their own oil before icing is applied.

How can I work with it if it's already happened?

If you've already got a cookie showing signs of butter bleed, roll with the punches. Put the cookie on a tray in the oven. Keep the oven off, and turn on just the oven light. After several hours, the subtle heat from the light bulb will reactivate the cookie's butter and make all the icing darker and even. No one will ever know the difference!

About the Author

Morgan Beck is a baker and graphic artist specializing in decorated sugar cookies. She studied graphic design at Iowa State University and has been a self-taught baker since 2015. She loves combining her design skills with her baking passion to create unique pieces of delicious art. She now runs her own baking business, Desserts and Stuff Bakery, and makes tens of thousands of custom cookies each year. She has been commissioned by several authors, publishing companies, and local businesses to create works of cookie art.

When she doesn't have a tablet pen or a piping bag in hand, Morgan loves walking her corgis, taking her boat out for fishing trips, and watching old movies with a cup of hot chocolate (no matter the season). She lives in the charming town of Woodstock, Illinois. Her work can be found at dessertsandstuffbakery.com.

Supplies and Resources

Meringue Powder and Edible Ink Markers
Chefmaster • www.chefmaster.com

Gel Food Color
AmeriColor • www.americolorcorp.com

Extracts
Watkins • www.watkins1868.com

Scribe Scraper Tool
Genie • www.stencilgenie.com

Silicone Scraper Tool
Genie • www.stencilgenie.com

Edible Ink Pens
tweets ... cookie connection • www.tweetscookieconnection.com/shop

Silicone Cookie Mats
Chua Cookie • chuacookie.com

Gold and Silver Metallic Luster Dust
The Sugar Art • www.thesugarart.com